CONFESSING FOR

MONEY

by Peggy Fielding

AWOC.COM
Denton, Texas

2nd Edition, revised and updated - September 2005

ISBN: 0-937660-20-5

Visit the author's web site: www.PeggyFielding.com

ACKNOWLEDGMENTS

Many thanks to Jheri Fleet, my publicist; to Dan Case, my electronic wizard; to the people who offered some clever ideas for cartoons; (I drew all the silly little pictures scattered throughout the book) and to my writer friend Jackie King, who can not only add and subtract. She can also multiply and divide as well...not to mention what she can do with Pie are Squared (or rounded) when she has a bushel of fruit.

"I WRITE WHENEVER I CAN, EVEN WHEN I'M HIP DEEP IN ALLIGATORS"

TABLE OF CONTENTS

CHAPTER 1:
WHAT A CONFESSION IS AND WHAT IT IS NOT

According to my dictionary, one of the definitions of the word *confessions* is… "a voluntary admission by an individual who has learned his/her lesson the hard way." We'll accept that. It is also the secret short story market which is always buying, buying, buying.

WHO READS THESE MAGAZINES?

The confessions we'll be discussing in this book are the same magazines that caused your grandmother to say to your mother, "Don't bring those magazines into this house." They are now published by the Dorchester Media, L.L.C. and they usually sit together in the drug store or grocery store or convenience store magazine rack. Four of them are directed to the white female: True Confessions, True Story, True Romance and True Love. Six are for the black female: Black Confessions, Black Romance, Black Secrets, Bronze Thrills, Jive and True Black Experience. The two groups are fairly different in content. The main differences you'll notice at the newsstand will appear in the color of the models who pose for the illustrations for the stories and for the color of the pretty woman on the cover. Payment is a bit less at the Black Confessions.

Your mother paid attention to your grandmother in a certain way. She didn't bring the confessions home but she continued to read them, nevertheless, at the beauty shop, at school, or at the houses of her friends whose mothers read the magazines and saw no reason why their daughters and friends shouldn't read them.

These days, girls and women of all ages are still reading them, particularly the blue collar or pink collar workers or wives of blue collar workers. (Pink collar workers are women who work at traditional women's jobs which do not require the worker to get dirty... secretaries, hair stylists, cashiers, store clerks, day care workers, etc.)

NO LONGER SIN, SUFFER AND REPENT

Your grandmother was wrong when she forbade your mother to read confessions. At the time she told your mother that, the stories were not just stories of sexual misbehavior as grandma suspected, they were quite moral stories which told stories of girls who sinned, of girls who suffered for their sins, and of girls who repented of their sins and then lived happily ever after because they had done the right things.

Few modern confessions follow the sin, suffer and repent formula of yesterday but these magazines are still highly moral in outlook and presentation. Generally speaking they demonstrate common American values, the things most American women hold dear such as a lifetime marriage plan, family interaction, care for others, family closeness, etc. Nearly every story is about some young, middle aged or older female's problem of the moment and how she handles it wrong, then how she faces the problem and herself and overcomes whatever is bothering her. Few of the protagonists in these stories are male but editors do like to buy an occasional male viewpoint story. Today's confession magazines are in the aid, service, and education business.

ONE PERSON'S PROBLEM AND HOW SHE/HE HANDLES IT

It's true that today's stories don't focus on "sin, suffer and repent," although there are still a few of that type. The disgrace of the illegitimate child has gone the way of all flesh. Sorry. But hey! We still have a world of problems, don't we? What is a problem to a middle class intellectual writer can also be a problem to a confessions heroine. (Except for the problem of getting published, perhaps.)

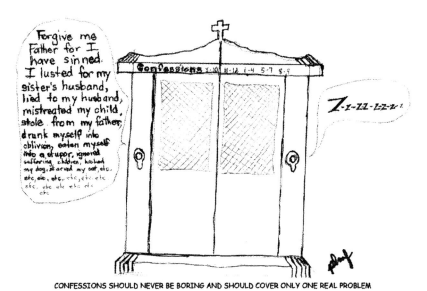

CONFESSIONS SHOULD NEVER BE BORING AND SHOULD COVER ONLY ONE REAL PROBLEM

Perhaps since modern mores are a great deal more accepting of unmarried sex, children born out of wedlock, divorce, and other so-called "sins" of the 1940s and 50s, there are still a few sins for our heroines to jump into even today.

Our confessions are about today's women's problems. We write about one problem per story. Too many beginning writers think they must load all of their protagonist's problems into one story... but that doesn't work. Modern readers want to learn about the heroine's one problem that is now bothering her, one problem and how she got into that mess, how she handles it, and finally, how everything turns out okay for her... or at least how she looks forward to a hopeful future. Readers of these stories believe them to be true stories and they *are* based upon real happenings in today's world. Many a wife has discovered that her husband, ol' Bubba, has been sniffing cocaine, so if you sit down and write a story of such a wife and tell how she handled the problem, you're writing a story based on a true happening, aren't you? And by helping your narrator to solve the story problem you're helping your readers find a way to handle their own cocaine sniffing Bubbas.

IMPLICIT MORAL VALUES OUR READERS HOLD

The moral of the story (what our narrator learns) should not be pointed out directly as authors used to do in the old days. We need to write today's story with the implicit moral underscored by what our characters say, do and think.

What are the morals (values) most clearly demonstrated in confessions? There are several and every story demonstrates one or more of them.

Those implicit morals are:

- Shacking up is okay but legal marriage is much better.

- Marriage without children is okay but legal marriage with two or more children is infinitely better.

- A child born out of wedlock is okay but being born a child to loving (married) parents is a thousand times better.

- Practicing no religion is okay but attending church occasionally is better: Attending an established church consistently and taking part in the church activities is the best of all possible worlds.

- Getting government help to live is okay if there is no other way, but working and caring for your own by the sweat of your brow is ever so much better.

- Leaving your children in childcare is okay but being a stay-at-home-mother, although seldom possible, is top-of-the-trees better.

- Sending sick, older or disabled family members to an institution to be cared for by others is okay but to care for your own loved one within your family is the really correct way to handle such problems if you can manage to do so.

In other words, our readers have accepted without question the middle class American values of *Father, Mother, and two kids all living in a loving home where the extended family works and attends church and takes part in community activities together.*

WHY WRITE CONFESSIONS?

If you're determined to write short fiction this may be a good field for you. Confessions need to be based on fact but if you can sign the publisher's contract, "Based on fact" with a good heart, then you can write confessions and make some money with your short stories. Our readers consider all the stories in our magazines to be truthful transcripts of what happened to our main characters so keep mum outside the writing community, best not to say that the confessions are made-up stories based on life's realities. That's why I like to call the confessions our *secret short story market.*

Sure it's true.
I read it in my
True Confession

There is a catch. You must study the confessions markets. See what the editors are looking for. Genre fiction, which is a fancy fiction writer word for category material, is what we're dealing with here. You do have to quit listening to your mother or your English teacher screaming inside your head and just march yourself right up to the nearest magazine rack and buy an assortment of the magazine. They have names like *True Confessions*, *True Romance*, *Bronze Thrills*, but you're not through yet. You must read the magazines back to front, then come up with a character, usually a blue collar worker or wife of a blue collar worker and then give her a problem. Then you'll be ready to write.

While you continue to try to perfect your commercial slick magazine short story, your romance novel, your mid-list woman's fiction, your literary bestseller, you can, at the same time, be working up to that prestigious sale and practicing your art right now by driving in the category lane as a confession writer and you can make a little money while you're doing it. Of course, you do want money for your work don't you?

You've heard what the Victorian literary light, Dr. Johnson said, haven't you? He said, "Only a blockhead would write for anything but money."

Remember... one problem, a wrong choice or two and, finally, your narrator finds her way out of the maze and looks at the future with hope. Sound easy? It's not, but it is do-able...and if you do it right you can start cashing checks.

No byline, just money and publication.

CHAPTER 2: HOW TO BECOME A CONFESSION STORY WRITER

Charles Dickens gave really useful advice for confession writers when he said, "Make them laugh, make them cry, make them wait." We can do that.

PUT YOUR LONGTERM DREAMS ON HOLD

You may have decided some time ago that you wanted to be a short story writer. If you really want to be a short story writer you'll need to read short stories. Try to get hold of the commercial or literary magazines that may be the markets for the type of story you want to write.

Published short stories are your textbooks. You'll need to read them and analyze them. There is no shame in modeling your first few stories on stories that have been published. We all learn from our predecessors' efforts in whatever field. We all stand on the shoulders of those who have gone before us.

Of course, Poe and Hemingway and Fitzgerald are all wonderful but you need to be reading and modeling your work on the short stories of present day writers just to keep yourself in the modern current. You are writing for a different world than Faulkner occupied. Look at Joyce Carol Oates or Robert Love Taylor if you want to be a literary light. Read the short story writers in the current Redbook, Playboy, Good Housekeeping, Women's World and other slick magazines if you want to be a commercial short story writer. The literary short stories and the commercial short stories live in two separate countries and never the twain shall meet.

But the good news that this book brings you is that you can start your short story writing career in another way. You can start writing for the *hidden market for short stories*, the market which buys and keeps on buying, even though you're a beginner. I'm suggesting you practice your writing in the more accessible market, that is, the confession market. There are 10 magazines in the Dorchester Media group of confessions. All are waiting for a story from you. All you must do is write to their particular specifications.

SURVEY THE MARKET

If you're determined to write fiction, short or long, you can do it. You *can* break into the marketplace with fiction and you *can* make some money doing it. But there is a catch. You must study your market and you really must come down from your ivory tower.

What kind of fiction are most publishers searching for? Genre Fiction, which is a fancy writer word for saying they want fiction that falls within a category which they publish. Mystery, science fiction, westerns, adventure, romance and confessions are all "genre" or category stories. If you really love a good mystery and you're willing to study the market and learn how to write a mystery story, you will, with persistent effort, be able to sell your mystery short story. The same is true for the other categories.

Short fiction has categories that are reasonably easy to break into. The easiest are the short mystery, the inspirational/ religious short, the romance short story and easiest of all, the confession. Confessions are easier to sell because there are more magazines that buy them. While you continue to try to perfect your commercial slick magazine short story or your literary short-short story, you can practice your art right now by studying the confessions market. Studying the market means you must buy and read the magazines from front to back, including ads, letters, poems, cartoons, and articles. That is the first step to becoming a knowledgeable confessions story writer.

GET THE RIGHT TOOLS

You must have a typewriter, word processor or computer to make it as a writer. The computer will make your writing life ten times easier and more productive but don't think that you can't write confessions and sell them from your typewriter. You can still do that. It is just a bit more difficult to work that way than with a computer.

Other tools you'll need will be reams of good 18 or 20 pound bond paper, metal paper clips and business sized envelopes as well as manila 9x12 envelopes, and blank computer discs to copy your stories to. You need a really good, first rate, dictionary. More than one couldn't hurt. You need to lay your hands on a King James version of the Bible. I'm not trying to make you into a religious writer, it's just that daily reading of a tiny bit of the oldest available version of our language helps you improve your own English. If you can't bear the thought of having a Bible in your house get a volume of Shakespeare and read a tiny bit of that material each day before you start work. You'll also need a volume of *The Elements of Style* by Strunk and White which you also need to dip into each day. I keep my copy in the bathroom. Become a master of our wonderful language.

There are other books that are essential to your well being as a writer, such as *Rodales' Synonym Finder* I turn to my copy nearly every day. It is so much easier to use than a thesaurus. You also need to have the new *Writer's Market* which comes out in October each year. You can get the electronic version and *Writer's Digest*, publisher of the volume, now keeps that electronic version up-to-date by the month. The electronic version is a bit more expensive than the traditional volume. I am a dinosaur so I prefer the printed version which is updated each year in September and the print version costs less than electronic version. A serious writer cannot be without this particular book. It is a market list giving addresses, what the publishers are looking for, whether the magazine takes fiction or nonfiction and what the editors want to see from you. Don't expect to use a *Writer's Market* for more than one year, It becomes obsolete very soon after you buy it because the publishing business is always in a state of flux. Without question you'll want to have your very own copy of the book you are now reading, *Confessing for Money*, which you can order from AWOCBooks.com for $14.95 (plus S&H). You may also wish to hear my *Confessing for Money* tape from Timberwolf Press (http://tinyurl.com/2zzfw).

FIND A TIME AND A PLACE FOR WRITING

People who make it in the writing business are the ones who hit their computer/typewriter keys every day for a specified length of time... at a particular hour of the day. They always go to the place they've chosen as their "writing place."

WRITE EVERY DAY

Writing every day is the way to make it in the writing business, confessions included. Not only do selling writers write every day, they send out what they write. They send their work to a contest or an editor or an agent. Of course, agents aren't interested in trying to sell your confessions but after you've had some successes you may wish to start writing books and that is when you will be able to find an agent to help you in your business. The agent is way on down the line for us when we've just begun our confessions careers.

WRITE IN ONE SITTING IF POSSIBLE

Successful writers keep on doing these two things over and over and over no matter how discouraged we may feel at the New York editor's rejection of our fine confession stories. We go to the same place every day at the same time and start work on our latest confession idea, then we finish it and send it out. It is a good idea to do your first draft in one sitting, if possible. That makes for continuity within the story.

EDIT WHEN COLD

Pouring out your story onto the page the first time around is the hot work. Thrilling, but I think cold work is even more fun. That is when you go over the structure you've built in the heat of a moment and you make repairs, additions and deletions. The rewriting is a bit like working on a puzzle some writers think. Most confessions need at least three rewrites to become publishable stories. If you do a lot more rewriting you are making yourself work for almost no money even if you sell your story.

CHAPTER 3: LEARN MANUSCRIPT PREPARATION

I confess I'm using the tools that I have, my head and my hands and the part that I sit on. (Too much of that to show on this page!)

Now for the hard work. In order to be considered a professional by editors, agents or contest judges, writers should follow correct manuscript format. If you wish to see what *Writers Market* recommends turn to their table of contents.

There are few set-in-concrete rules for manuscript formatting other than the law of using common sense. Many editors have told me they look for overall appearance. Neatness, beauty, and correct spelling, all count with judges, editors and agents.

PAPER/PAPERCLIPS, ENVELOPES, STAMPS

You'll need a typewriter or a computer and printer, preferably the latter. Your printer must roll out print that is easily read, both large enough and clear enough to pass through the readers' eyes without difficulty. Use nothing smaller than a 12-point font. Use Courier, Helvetica, or Times New Roman or something similar. Editors want to see a simple typewritten looking sort of print that offers caps and lower case letters.

You will need 18 to 20 pound white bond paper and good quality #10 white envelopes as well as 9x12 manila, white, or gray envelopes for mailing your confessions. Train your local post office people to bring out interesting stuff when you ask for stamps. Interesting stamps may help you just the slightest bit because of the fact that so many people in the mailrooms of publishing houses collect stamps. They may want yours and perhaps the mailroom person will load your confession on top of the pile so he can have first dibs on your great looking stamps. Stamps bought through your computer will do the job, of course, but they aren't eye-catching and I don't think anyone is collecting them these days (as yet.) The same goes for postal machines. They make neat postage but their machine made or electronic-print-looks probably aren't attractive to the mailroom boy.

A few paper clips, the silvery looking ones, and you'll be in business. Put your clip to the left, topside of your page, slanting toward the left a bit. I have had a well-known New York editor say to me, "If the paper clip isn't in the right place I don't bother with the piece. I just put it into the SASE and ship it back." In other words, the writer wasn't being a professional when he or she put the clip in the center or on the right or any other place than the top left hand corner of the cover page. That statement was a wake-up call for me. This isn't just an arbitrary decision on the part of readers and editors. They want to hold your stuff with their left hand while flipping through your story with the right. See? Every direction I give you in this book has some sort of reasonable justification behind it. For example: metal paper clips hold materials better than do rubberized colored clips. Did you know that? So be smart. Use metal ones.

FORMAT

The first rule of manuscript format that we must follow is that double-spacing (no, not space and a half!) requirement and the necessary white space on the first page of every confession, as well as in the margins on every page. Judges and editors expect to use that white space for ease of reading as well as presenting a convenient place for their own notes.

Start every confession with your legal name, address and zip in the top left-hand corner of your first page, observing the 1 ¼" to 1 ½" margin. To the right corner of the first page, on the same line with your name, give the number of words in the story.

Go back to the left and double space after the zip. Give your email, FAX and telephone numbers. Don't bother with copyright symbols nor with what rights you are selling. Editors have told me that presenting this information irritates them. Respectable magazines copyright the whole magazine anyway, so you are protected.

Move a third to half way down the page and type the title of your confession in caps, centered on the line. Normally you would double space and put your byline centered under the story title but Confession magazines don't give us bylines for our short stories so no use putting your name under the title unless you just feel naked without it.

There is a third rule and that has to do with paragraphing. Double space or double space twice to begin your story, indenting five spaces for each new paragraph. At the end of your confessions story put a period or a question mark, whichever is suitable for your last sentence, and then nothing more. No 30 with a circle around it, no "The End," no cute little doodles, just a period or a question mark.

MAILING, SASE, EMAIL

Prepare to wait some long months (sometimes as long as eight months) before you hear from your editor at the confessions magazine you've chosen. You send the completed story to all of the magazines, then wait for your editor's reaction. All the editors want the completed story mailed to them via the US post office. Nowadays they also want a computer disc of the story along with the manuscript if you are able to furnish one. So send out your story and your SASE, (self addressed stamped envelope) then note in your record of the story where you sent it on what day. Time now to get busy on another project. Don't wait to hear on that story you've just submitted. If you become a selling writer for the confessions you may be able to depend on selling a story a month if you can turn out what they want every month or even every week if you're hot for writing. Turn your writing into your second job, or your primary job if you aren't working for a wage anywhere else.

I recently interviewed Nathasha Brooks-Harris for the emagazine called *Writing for DOLLARS!*, at the request of editor Dan Case there. He has agreed to allow the interview to be reprinted here.

NATHASHA BROOKS-HARRIS INTERVIEW

NATHASHA BROOKS-HARRIS INTERVIEW
by Peggy Fielding

Brooks-Harris is editor for Bronze Thrills, Black Romance, and now, True Confessions. She has taken over that magazine from Pat Byrdsong who has moved onto other work.

After receiving a journalism degree from Hunter College, Brooks-Harris worked on newspapers and music and beauty magazines. She spent sometime

as a gossip columnist but she
hated that. She would never
want to be gossip columnist
again because of our
litigious society. "Every
gossip columnist lays him or
herself open to being sued
these days," she explains.

Happily divorced, with no
children, she lives in
Brooklyn. She is not totally
immersed in her job as editor
because she also loves to write her own stories
and has had two books published, one, PANACHE,
from Domhan, received an Emma Award. The second,
in which she appears in an anthology called CAN
I GET AN AMEN published by BET Books, appeared
on Four Best-Seller lists, so she understands
our business from the writer's side of the desk
as well as from the editor's side.

Readers who want to write for the confessions
magazines should ask for guidelines for the
particular magazine via U. S. Mail. Enclose a
self-addressed #10 sized envelope for each set
of guidelines which interest you. Your requests
will be addressed in the following way

Bronze Thrills
Nathasha Brooks-Harris, Editor
Dorchester Media, LLC
33 Seventh Avenue, 11th Floor
New York, NY 10001

WFD: How do we submit stories for your three
magazines?

Brooks-Harris: That's easy. Write it and mail
the double spaced hard copy (typed) story with a

disc containing the material. 9x12 Manila SASE should be enclosed as well.

WFD: Can we submit stories to any of the black confessions group via e-mail?

NBH: Marcia Mahan will take e-mail materials if you make a special arrangement with her. All of us prefer hard copy, actually. Sometimes I telephone the writers if we need to discuss something in the story. I don't always do that but I do like to call sometimes since that is a quicker way to straighten out problems.

WFD: Should writers submit stories to all the confessions editors simultaneously? Multiple submissions in other words?

NBH: Oh, no. It's best to send each story to one editor at a time, although we do sometimes hand on a story to the magazine we think to be more in line with that type of story. It's best to submit a story to each editor, one at a time. No multiple submissions, please.

WFD: Does Dorchester Media LLD offer a website we may access?

NBH: Yes, Go to DorchesterMedia.com. It has just been updated.

WFD: You've talked a bit about themed issues. How can we learn what themes you have in mind for Black Romance and Bronze Thrills?

NBH: Just write and ask.

WFD: I loved the theme you used for Bronze Thrills and Black Romance recently, "Working girls connecting with Blue collar guys." Will you be doing themed issues for True Confessions, also?

NBH: I'm not sure.

WFD: I love the idea.

NBH: Writers can contact me for information about that. I do know it will be different for writers, sending hard copies to True Confessions, enclosing discs and learning the ways of the U.S. Mail.

WFD: How do you pay at Bronze Thrills and Black Romance.

NBH: We pay $100 per story and $100 for feature articles. If the story or article is a bit shorter, say four manuscript pages, we pay $50 for that size article or story. For poetry that we like we pay $2.00 a line. Payment is sent one month after the magazine hits the newsstand. We are a bit slow, in other words.

WFD: What length and what type of stories do you prefer for Bronze Thrills or Black Romance?

NBH: We like contemporary, entertaining and informative material. We're not looking for dreary stories or sadness. We want our characters to triumph in the end, although bittersweet (hope for the future) endings are okay. We'd like to see 14 to 16 pages.

WFD: Tell us what kinds of stories in particular that you are looking for in Bronze Thrills right now.

NBH: I like a story that holds my interest, perhaps the Chik-Lit type of story, where our narrator struggles with her job, her man, and life-in-the-city. Universally, these are usually stories for women. We do look for romance. Remember Dynasty? We like stories of that type which could be used in an ongoing serialized story which might cover two or three or four months.

WFD: And for Black Romance?

NBH: In that magazine we like to go through a bit of drama, particularly the "making-up-scenes."

WFD: As for sex?

NBH: We use erotic, tasteful erotica. We don't use "the shocking words." We like the sex scene done with style and romance. Both Bronze Thrills and Black Romance stories *must* include one sex scene which is an integral part of the story.

WFD: How about seasonal stories? How far ahead should we submit to Bronze Thrills and Black Romance for Christmas, Kwanzaa? Chanukah? New Years Eve? New Years Day? Three Kings? Cinco de Mayo?

NBH: We love them right now. I'm seriously interested in stories of Black Jews for Chanukah and Hispanic stories using Three Kings or Cinco de Mayo. By the way, settings are important. Take the stories out of New York City and California. We get way too much of those places.

WFD: Do we need to label the outside envelope to let you know this story is for a specific holiday?

NBH: Oh, yes. Please label and sent at least six months ahead of the holiday. This goes for True Confessions, also.

WFD: How about special interest months such as school openings, graduation, June Brides, Groundhog Day, etc., do you want those labeled as well?

NBH: Yes, for all three magazines. Please label and send six months before the month or time of that event. For instance a story set in National Rodeo Month (November) would really tempt us!

WFD: Are there specific articles written for Bronze Thrills?

NBH: Yes. Bronze Thrills likes nonfiction that is inspirational for our "Keep the Faith" section. We recently ran a piece called "How to Recommit To Your Spouse." Then there is "Seductively Speaking," and "Sexual Health," columns.

We like love, marriage, dating, romance, dealing with partners, dropping partners, any nonfiction advice in those fields. Men into the "down low" topic is especially hot for stories right now.

WFD: Must we be black to write for Bronze Thrills or Black Romance?

NBH: No. You only need to be a romantic fanatic.

WFD: Do authors have input as to cover art or illustrations for stories?

NBH: No.

WFD: Do we receive bylines?

NBH: Not for stories. We give bylines for articles and poetry only.

WFD: Where can we find Bronze Thrills and Black Romance magazine for study?

NBH: Wal-Mart, Rite Aid, Books-A-Million, Grocery Stores/convenience stores/gas stations in black neighborhoods.

WFD: Can we subscribe?

NBH: You can subscribe by calling 1-800-666-8783, which is an outside subscription service, and of course, each magazine has subscription cards enclosed.

WFD: How many pieces do you acquire for each month?

NBH: Between two and four Nonfiction features, eleven confession stories and one mini erotic story for Bronze Thrills. If you want to do a long serialization please query by mail as to your intentions.

WFD: How about the male POV for Bronze Thrills or Black Romance?

NBH: Yes. I will be accepting a few Males POV confessions and feature articles. It's great to hear from the men and we're interested in what they have to say. We've always had a few male POV stories in True Confessions.

WFD: Anything else writers need to know?

NBH: Keep writing. Never give up. Every real writer should send out one or two pieces every

week. Even writers who are successful will write
for us. Alex Haley was a regular writer for True
Confessions. His wife left him because of his
confessions writing.

CHAPTER 4: WHAT SHALL I WRITE ABOUT IN MY CONFESSION STORIES?

There are millions of stories out there. All women (and all men) have problems. What we do is write about them, one at a time. I suggest you keep a notebook in your pocket or purse so that whenever you see or hear of a particular problem that interests you, you'll just jot that down in your notebook. This is your future confessions storage bin. You'll thank yourself for that one of these days.

STOCK SITUATIONS AND OLD STANDBYS

There are several story lines that have been used ever since these magazines have been on the stands. We can still use them, just putting a modern spin on the solving of the problem. The

31

three most used problems have been death, divorce or disaster...
either manmade or God given. We just need to look at the problem from our modern narrator's point-of-view and help her solve
her problem as today's woman would.

Other standbys that have been shown in many a confession
magazine are love stories, inspirational stories, child/children
problems and the problems of older persons such as parent or
grandparent inserted into our narrator's life. The love story, or
more aptly, the deprivation-of-love from our narrator, has always
been, hands down, the editor's and reader's favorite story type.

Newer trends taken straight from the headlines, such as AIDS,
abortion questions, broken faith in God because of disil-
lusionment, war and of course, terrorism and terrorists, can be
used as the germ of the problem faced by the narrator in your
story.

Funny is okay too, at most of the magazines, but harder to sell
because what is funny to me may not be funny to my editor. There
are also the documentary type stories where our heroine describes

a legal process, a new medical technology, a legal angle on a family problem, or the pressure of community or family custom. If you use customs or usages or processes within your local legal or political scene be sure that the same type of organization or layout is more or less the same nationally. If you don't know, contact your local officials and ask!

For example, in one story I had my young woman solve a problem by forming an all-woman softball team which entered the softball league team schedules set up by the Tulsa Park Department. Good news! I found that most small cities and large, have a similar softball league set up, with practice and scheduled games organized and posted by the parks or games departments in city and state competitions. I used Tulsa's set up without being too specific, realizing that usually most confessions editors change the location of every story they buy for your sake as well as for their own protection. In other words, be a little generic in your approach to this type of story. Make sure there is such a custom, organization, institution, political entity, etc. in most other parts of the U.S.A. A Bail Bondsman in Tulsa is probably much like a Bail Bondsman in Atlanta or Seattle but a religious organization may offer one type of service in Houston and quite a different service in New York City. You need to find out what the differences are.

National organizations and country wide 800 numbers also provide material for confession writers. They provide not only a problem (such as the national cocaine hotline) but a variety of solutions as well, in most cases. What people have done across the country to help their learning disabled children to do well in school requires only that you get in touch with what was once called ACLD (Association for Children with Learning Disabilities) and is now called ALD, which allows the inclusion of high schoolers, college students and other adults who might suffer from this widespread learning problem. Each variety of problem such as dyslexia, dysgraphia, directional difficulties, etc. are treated in different manners. The sufferers are usually smart and terribly creative. They just learn in a different way than most students. For example, Cher suffers from dyslexia. No one can accuse that lady of being dumb or uncreative. The national organization can answer all your questions at no cost except postage, or phone tolls or a little time on the internet. Or you can visit a meeting of your local chapter of the national organization where you can talk to LD students or their parents. Remember writers; hands-on research is always the better way to find out about your narrator's problem.

THE MOST COMMON FORMULA FOR CONFESSIONS STORIES IN TODAYS MAGAZINES

I hope using the word formula doesn't set your teeth on edge. Using the word "formula" just means that you are using an outline that will appeal to your confessions magazine editor. It isn't copying or ripping off other writers or being trite or unoriginal. All writing follows a formula of one sort or another. The formula we use actually allows you more freedom to write while keeping you in the ballpark where confessions are played. The most common formula may read something like the following:

1. A woman presents her problem, usually within the first two or three paragraphs of the story. This is the point at which our narrator faces her problem and decides she must take action.

2. Within the first few paragraphs after she has faced her problem, our narrator gives us some of the background of her problem. In these few paragraphs we learn of the narrator's "flaw" or inherent weakness or her motivation for handling her problem, stemming from her past. She tells us what led up to this problem which she is now facing and we also learn why she is reacting this way. Sometimes we have an actual "flashback" although editors aren't so crazy about flashbacks as they once were.

3. Based on the previous information, our heroine makes a wrong decision. That bad choice sets up a chain of events which seems to put our girl into a hopeless situation.

4. The hopeless situation causes her to react and make another decision where she decides to act in a different manner and to make a different (better) choice.

For a much longer story you may wish to have your narrator make two or more wrong choices, one after the other, before finally coming up with the right choice.

5. After making what will turn out to be the right choice, a suspenseful climax is reached because she made that particular turn in the road. During this section of the story, the concluding scene in your story, a statement of the theme or suggestion that life will be brighter in the future wraps up the happy ending or the bittersweet ending (bittersweet means everything isn't great right now but there is a light at the end of the tunnel and life will get better on down the road.) Complete hopelessness and despair can work in your literary short story but they have absolutely no place in a confession story conclusion. These stories are written to give help, hope and an understanding of life as it is lived today, to our readers.

ANOTHER COMMON STORY FORMULA WHICH INCORPORATES AN OUTSIDE FACTOR OR TWO

The "outside factor" which your narrator meets in this kind of story may be put upon her by some outside force. She then solves her problem using another outside factor to help her solve her problem. This formula goes something like this:

1. Our narrator meets a problem which has been dumped upon her by fate or by custom or law or by someone else,

such as a family member. She resents this problem and may try to ignore it.

2. Trying to ignore the problem leads to more and more difficulties for our girl.

3. Our narrator suffers because it is impossible to ignore this particular problem. She must face the consequence of her wrong choice (when she turned her back on the problem) and she must come up with another way of handling the problem.

4. She solves the problem on her own, usually with a germ of information or a seed of education available to her when she reaches out for it. She usually sacrifices in some way to solve this problem, but the sacrifice is something she can live with, of course.

5. Our heroine (or hero) learns something from this experience and begins to look to the future where everything will be better for her or him (as well as for his or her family.) Sometimes a male protagonist can work well in this type of story. That does not mean that a male narrator can't be used in any of the other stories. It's just that editors usually prefer female protagonists. Very often the concluding paragraphs of this type of story points in some way back to the title or the hook in the opening paragraphs which originally drew us into the story.

GETTING IDEAS FOR THE OUTSIDE FACTOR(S) TO USE IN OUR STORIES

The newspapers, soap operas, TV news shows, advice columns, new laws, religious rules and community customs, as well as a list of 800 numbers to call for help, will give you great ideas for writing this type of story where our narrator is put upon by someone or something else. You may be able to order a booklet listing 800 numbers that people from all across the country can call for immediate crisis intervention, help or information referrals. Ask for the 800 numbers listings when you send $2.00 to Hotlines, Adelphi University School of Social Work, Box 703, Garden City, NY 11530.

You could also develop your own private list as gleaned from newspapers, TV shows, magazine stories, your friends' troubles and other sources.

"... AND I KIND OF ENJOY LIVING ALONE, BUT THANKS ANYWAY."

His identity has to remain a secret, of course, but I know one little Methodist Minister who has sold more than 200 confessions. Now where do you suppose he gets his story ideas?

And of course, there is always the Internet.

CONFESSION TABOOS

We tiptoe around certain problems. Some of the things I'll mention are really taboos, others need delicate handling. Walk carefully when writing about the following subjects:

Homosexuals, lesbians, even bisexuals are people, not social outcasts, but you must handle the problem gently and with great understanding of the situations in which they find themselves. It really would be better (more salable) if your narrator is straight and her husband, child, parent, sister or brother is the homosexual or bisexual.

Abortion is sometimes necessary but not always. Be sensitive here.

Unlimited promiscuity by our heroine is frowned upon. Our narrator must be a sympathetic character. Secondary Characters can sleep around if called upon to do so by the storyline.

Drug stories for our protagonists are out. Her man can be a druggie... her children or her parents can be druggies but we won't want to read about her if she is drugged out. Alcohol problems are a bit more okay for our protagonists if you feel you must write about this problem. I wouldn't care to have a drunken narrator on my desk or in my computer but you must decide this for yourself.

There is not much horror these days in interracial marriage so steer around this as a problem. It isn't.

Rebellious protagonists such as nuns, priests, preachers, etc. might better be left alone, although today's headlines have given us a little leeway in casting a priest as a bad guy. This story will not be told from the priest's point of view.

Straight incest is out for our narrator. No father-daughter, mother-son, brother-sister, etc. Now, a new stepfather (mother) or foster father (mother) can come on as a villain but they must get their comeuppance by story end. Our narrator simply "forgiving" the dirty guy is not enough. He (or she) badperson, must receive real punishment, preferably at the hands of our narrator and don't be afraid to call in the police or juvenile aid officials.

CHAPTER 5: RESPECT YOUR GENRE, YOURSELF AND YOUR FANS

Occasionally when I am teaching the class called "Confessing for Money" at the local Community college or speaking at a writers' workshop, I issue the commandment, "Go to a local store and buy some of these confession magazines. Try to get at least one of each of the lines. Send in subscriptions to the ones you think you'd like best." Invariably, two or more people in the class will shiver, sometimes look at a friend with the "I will never do that," look in their eyes and I am sure that neither that person nor her friend will become selling confessions writers.

MOVE ON TO WRITING THAT YOU RESPECT

If that is the way you feel, if you think your grandmother was right when she said, "Don't bring those magazines into this house," then you might as well put this book down now and move on to the kind of writing that suits you better. A person who denigrates the magazines for which she writes demonstrates that she has no respect for the genre, nor for the readers of confessions magazines. She also has no respect for herself as a writer if she looks down on the writing of these stories but plans to do so just in order to "be able to make some money." You must be a serious writer in order to write for this genre, serious in that you appreciate the magazines and you read them and you write for them with interest... with no shame, either publicly or privately.

CONFESSIONS FANS

There is some good news in this area and some advice I can share with you. Confessions readers are the best fans in the world. That is for sure. They read avidly, they cry, they laugh, they live your stories right along with your narrator and her friends and family. And they prove themselves to be the best of fans by writing to the narrator. Yes, we know the heroine you've written about exists only in your mind and on the page, but to our readers our story characters are real and our readers write to us through our characters, sometimes on tear stained note paper because they've been touched by Karen's, Sharon's, Jennifer's, Brandi's, or Rachel's story.

Readers often demonstrate true sisterhood with your characters, explaining how they solved that very problem or thanking Karen, Sharon, Jennifer, Brandi, or Rachel for giving them the information or tools to solve their own problems. Now folks, I promise you that won't happen to you when you sell your story to the New Yorker Magazine or even to Good Housekeeping. Someone may like your story and tell the editor so, but no one will write to your main character with such fervent interest and true devotion. I love every fan letter. I am sorry that the confessions have cut down somewhat on the printing of fan letters. To me those letters are the second best thing about the magazine, our stories being first, of course.

To me, the best part of selling a story to *True Love* or any of the other magazines (other than cashing the check, of course) always comes in the second or third month after the story appears and the readers have had time to read and react with a letter addressed to my main character. I simply love that.

The cashier of the store from whom you purchase your magazines silently congratulates you for buying the confessions. You are one of her few customers who reads anything decent so far as she is concerned. These magazines are probably her favorite reading materials.

Now, I understand what you are saying when you resist telling your literary friends that you are writing for the confessions markets. Believe me, they are terribly jealous that you are cashing a check every month or every week from your writing, but their deep down snobbishness about the confession magazines has communicated itself to you. When these writers ask what you write, here is what you say, the truth, without making up any excuses. Say, "I'm writing and selling short fiction to women's magazines."

Of course, the next question will be "Which magazines?" And your answer will be, "Oh, whoever is paying. What's your latest project, Poopoo?" and get your pal going on what she or he is working on. They are much more interested in that wonderful subject than in the discussion of your work.

A good confession can be
catharsis for the reader
and for the writer.

YOUR WORK AMONG WRITERS

Now, for your real working writer friends you tell all. Confession stories are not bad news among writers. Everyone would like to sell to them but not everyone can write a salable confession story, so, just for fun, amuse the other writers with your latest titillating titles and always grab the check in the restaurant because, among working writers, you will probably have the most money.

NEEDING SOME DIALOGUE

Not everyone can internalize the tone, the texture, the idea of a confession story. Other writers, non confessions writers, will say of your first person story, if it is read aloud in your critique group, "Good story, but I think it needs some dialogue."

That's the tip-off as to why that person can't sell a story to the *Trues*. The whole story, from the beginning word to the last word *is* dialogue. It just isn't encased within quotation marks. Naturally, if you have your narrator talking with her mother, friend, husband, or dog, etc. within the story, then you encase their chunks of conversation in quotation marks just as is usual in other types of writing. The rest of the story is her (your narrator) talking, explaining everything to you, the reader, her best friend, who listens with interest to every word she tells you about her problem and about how she is trying to solve it. That's why we call her *our narrator*. The narrator is always the person telling the story. She's the one who is spinning the narrative. She's confessing! To you.

CHAPTER 6: WHAT YOU'LL NEED TO SUCCEED AT WRITING CONFESSIONS

If you follow a few basic guidelines for writing and selling to the confessions magazines, it should be only a matter of time and practice before you get to be a regular contributor to those magazines.

Confession writing got
me where I am today.

BASIC GUIDELINES

Here are some things you'll need to remember in order to succeed as a published confessions storywriter.

- A sympathetic narrator is all important. Your narrator must be someone with whom the reader can identify. Yes, she has flaws, weaknesses, even an unlikable aspect in some ways perhaps, but all these traits are

47

balanced by her good traits. She is a person readers can like, a person who is basically decent, a person with a problem. She is a good person who is dealing with one problem, her most *current* personal problem.

- A first person viewpoint is essential. Your narrator is telling her story through her own monologue, dialogue, action and inner speech (introspection). It's "I" all the way.

- The confession tone of voice must be maintained. This voice is best achieved by imagining you're sitting at a kitchen table telling your best friend all about what happened to fling you into this particular problem at this particular time in your life. The confessions tone is intimate, natural, filled with detail. The story is peppered with convincing dialogue between your narrator and her closest cohorts. Aside from the nuggets of dialogue scattered throughout your story, you need good monologue (narration of the story) and introspection (inner dialogue) to help promote reader sympathy, and, of course, you need some action.

- You may present a story flashback if necessary. I suggest you only use a flashback if it is short and if it is something that you feel is required to deepen the reader's understanding of your narrator's problem.

- Texture and hominess are required. Weave friends, family, church, job, neighborhood, the past, hopes for the future, fears, etc., into the story for believability. Clear details are important. If a child is sick, what is his illness? Is the family dog a mutt adopted from the pound or a purebred cocker spaniel that the narrator's mother gave her? Did our narrator make those blue organdy kitchen curtains trimmed with red rickrack?

Touches of hominess lend texture and background and authenticity to your story.

- The story must open with a hook. The first sentence should grab the reader's (editor's) attention. By the end of the first or at most at the end of the second paragraph, your reader should have a fairly good idea of what problem our narrator is facing and the reader (editor) should begin to have a clue as to how our narrator is planning to solve her problem, even though it might be clear that her first plan is palpably wrong. We folks in the know want her first choice of action to be a wrong choice!

- Make your story strong and readable, filled with drama and conflict. Don't skim over conflict or crisis scenes. Don't leave out the arguments and slaps (if any). Your storyline progresses in ascending waves. We want a few tears and more than a bit of hand wringing along the way. It is in the crisis scenes that you draw your reader (editor) into your narrator's world. Your reader (editor) becomes afraid that everything is lost but she really hopes that Karen, Sharon, Jennifer, Brandy or Cathy will come out on top, her problem solved through her own efforts, and her future looking bright or at least livable, with hope for the future. (By the way, don't worry about your characters' names or your particular setting, other than as useful tools for your vision as you are writing. Your editor will almost invariably change your character's names and your setting. Pray that the editor knows a tiny bit about geography. In a recent story of mine, "I Married a Terrorist," the editor put my girl in Arkansas, her family in New Mexico. Her uncle drove up to her place in half an hour! Not possible in real life. A trek to New Mexico from Arkansas takes some hard driving and an overnight stay along the way. I had set the entire story in Oklahoma, but what can you do? I cashed the check and hoped the readers weren't astounded by the uncle's quick trip of thousands of miles in half an hour.)

- Our narrator must act upon and solve whatever problem is facing her. There are no fairy godmothers in the confessions magazines. Readers (editors) feel cheated if a story if wrapped up with "then I realized," or "I just knew everything would be all right," or "I'd been rescued by my baby's father." Take your reader with you when your narrator faces her moment of truth. Let your readers feel, taste, smell, hear, see or touch whatever your narrator feels, tastes, smells, hears, sees or touches. This is your narrator's moment of truth. Let her tell about her triumph in such a way that it feels as if it is happening to the reader. You've certainly heard the old saying, "Show, don't tell." In confessions you tell and in the telling you *show* what is happening to your narrator.

- Try for a full circle or a satisfying ending. Sometimes we need to conclude with a projection into the future so the reader knows briefly what will happen with our narrator. Did she stay married? Did she learn to say, "no?" Did she begin to understand that not all men are bad? Etc. Or you can point back to the beginning in some way and tell how things are different now. It was raining when the story started and the problem was presented, and now the sun is shining and our narrator looks out the window and comments on the beauty of the sun. That's a full circle idea.

OUTLINING HELPS

When you are using one of the formulas to make an outline for a new story, it is good to remind yourself of the above rules and to try to insert a hint of your version of each rule into your new story outline. You'll find that outlining makes the writing much easier. Some people write their confessions by just jotting down whatever comes to mind and hoping for the best, but that is not the easy way. Too much rewriting is required when you try that seat-of-your-pants-type-flying through your story.

Jump into the story with a written plan in mind, just notes to yourself on scratch paper will do, and you'll find the writing of the actual story progresses much more quickly and easily.

An outline can be as simple as four or five sentences to remind you of what you've been thinking but for the inexperienced writer a more detailed outline may be more helpful. The full outline may start with character sketches of your main two or three characters, then a sentence or phrase telling something about each scene or perhaps something about each paragraph. An outline is just notes to yourself to help you write your story without getting too far off track. Here is an example of the sort of simple thing you might do for yourself to help you get started:

Cleo Reed has trouble with her eyes. She was once a beauty operator. Her husband of thirty years, Jim Bob, is a long distance truck driver. Their marriage is okay but a bit humdrum. She prays for a better life.

Cleo tries to ignore the eye problem, tries to pretend that nothing is happening to her, but she feels depressed. All she does is watch TV.

She has a problem driving her little car along places she hasn't been before. She begins to be afraid she may lose her license.

She goes to the Doctor and tells him her problem. He gives her a letter that says she would be fine driving locally from her house to the grocery store. She won't get any worse nor any better either, he tells her. She gets new, heavier glasses. She thinks she looks ugly but she doesn't do anything to better herself until the fear of the lack of the use of her car frightens her.

Cleo goes to talk to the license people and with her letter she is able to get a special license.

She begins to learn to appreciate audio books. She buys a big screen TV. She begins to feel better with her somewhat restricted life but she longs to feel useful. She doesn't want to spend the rest of her days just watching TV and listening to audio books.

She prays to God to find a way to let her accomplish something in this world.

She thinks about getting a job and discusses that plan with Jim Bob when he comes home. As they talk they work around to the idea of Cleo having her own beauty shop.

Jim Bob, with Cleo's help, builds a small beauty salon space on the back of the house for the neighborhood ladies and former clients who still want her attention. Soon she has more work than she can handle. Since she is in the public eye she begins to pay more attention to her own appearance.

She decides to quit letting the work keep her from things she wants to do and cuts the salon hours to afternoons only. Her working life gives her more vibrancy and energy thus making her more interesting to Jim Bob. She and husband work out a plan that she will travel with him for a few days every third weekend if he has to be driving. They do this so they can get reacquainted.

See? Simple. One problem. She does wrong things twice. (Ignores her bad sight and leans on audio books and large screen TV too much.) Then she really asks God for help and works out her problem which is not that she has eye troubles but that she lacks self esteem and thinks there isn't anything she can do to better her life. She pulls herself up by her own bootstraps with God's blessings and a little help from good old Jim Bob.

BUSINESS MATTERS ARE IMPORTANT FOR CONFESSIONS WRITERS

There are other things you must do as confession writers and they mostly concern the business of writing. One of the things that you must do is keep records of what you are doing. Keep them either in a notebook or on 3 by 5 cards or electronically in your computer. Keep a list of submissions and how and where you sent your story and on what date. You must also note what happened to each submission. This is for your benefit and also for the Internal Revenue Service (IRS) tax collector.

Bookkeeping is essential. That means keeping track of money spent and money earned. The IRS will surely be interested in this. You may, with no problem at all, take off many of your expenditures as legal write-offs, the cost of doing business. Save written records of payments, checks, and receipts for at least six years, just in case.

Write-offs you may need to claim: All office supplies (paper, pens, pencils, staples, paperclips, ink, rubber bands, etc.) Office equipment can also be written off but you'll need to decide how to do this after discussing it with your accountant. You can also write off the cost of every newspaper subscription, every magazine subscription or purchase, every book you buy, all tapes and CD's as well as rental or purchase price of all movies or documentary films. This is wonderful news for readers like us. Think of every printed or pictured word that passes through your eyes or ears and into your brain, as *market research*. Hurrah! I have always spent more money on books and magazines than I have on clothing or shelter. Personally, I think this is such a great write-off that I increase my book buying whenever I so much as think about the fact that all books are write-offs for me (and for all writers).

You can also write off library fees, classes in writing or classes in related subjects such as English, grammar, literature, computer usage, photography or even art classes if you are drawing to illustrate any of your written work. (You don't illustrate your confessions with drawings or photographs. The editor or her design person attends to that, but in case of writing nonfiction, poetry or some literary short fiction, black and white illustrations and/or photographs or transparencies are often welcomed.) Go to conferences and conventions and workshops to learn your craft and write off the costs. Just don't overdo. You have to spend a big chunk of your time writing, you know.

If you take a trip to look over a small town, you can write off the expense of such research if you can show your story attempts are set in small towns, or the mountains or cities, or you name it. You can take off half of your food or entertainment costs if you are researching a story or trying to show your editor or agent a good time during your conference. Yep, that's half off whenever you are treating your writing VIP to dinner and dancing, etc. Sorry, your spouse's or lover's or children's expenses cannot be written off. Look for a more detailed discussion of this business stuff in Chapter 12.

CHAPTER 7: STORY EMOTIONS

There are lots of emotions which you may use in your stories but there are about seven emotions that are the stock-in-trade of our confessions. Many others, such as grief, jealousy, or humor, can come into play upon occasion. However the hands-down favorite emotion, as expressed by editors and thousands of readers is the first on our list. Most stories offer at least five of the seven favorite emotions and some stories contain all seven.

You've probably already guessed the most favored emotion? *Love?* You were right, of course.

LOVE

Our stories deal with all sorts of love but man-woman love is the all around favorite, especially when it concerns the fact that one or the other of our main characters is deprived of love. When real love (or the expectation of real love) comes to your narrator through some action on her part, the battle is won and our story ends happily or at least it ends with your narrator expecting happiness in the near future.

Your narrator doesn't always have to be the person deprived of love nor does the deprivation have to be from a man. Your narrator can be depriving someone else of love. She can reject her child because he is mentally retarded or handicapped in some other way. You might make the story theme for such a situation be the fact that her rejection of the child is affecting her love life with her husband.

A story using deprivation of love as its theme appeared in *True Story.* Frieda, married, middle-aged, has only her Mom as her confidante and her closest friend. Mom dies. Frieda insists that her 70-year-old Papa come to live with her and her husband Max. Frieda thinks Papa really needs her. In reality, it's Frieda who needs Papa as a substitute for her close relationship with Mom.

Frieda spends so much time trying to make Papa happy in her home that she doesn't realize she is neglecting her husband, Max.

When Papa finds a widow and decides to remarry, Frieda does everything in her power to stop the wedding (Wrong choices, you see!).

An older relative talks to Frieda and makes her answer some hard questions. The questions force her to realize what her preoccupation with her Papa is doing to her own marriage. She finally takes the right steps and all ends happily.

Confessions stories aren't just stories of men pursuing women or vice versa. They are tales of love lost and love found between people of all ages, whether parent and child, husband and wife, sister and sister, etc.

SEX

Now the idea of sex in all confessions is the stereotyped idea of what confessions magazines are about. Just realize that titles on the cover have been a bit lurid to promote sales. That's why your grandmother said, "Don't bring those magazines into this house!" She had a naughty mind and her own idea (usually totally incorrect) of what our stories are all about. Nowadays, titles are softened and we are dropping the subtitles

Up until the 1970's, confessions stories didn't even have titillating scenes. A man about to make love romantically, picked up the heroine, carried her to the bedroom... and kicked the door shut.

What followed this door kicking was only implied because the next paragraph started with a transition such as, "Later we..." The activities which took place in the space between the closed door and "Next morning..." all happened in Grandmother's sexed-up little mind.

SORROW

Dickins, talking about editors purchasing a writer's work, said it first, I think, and editors still abide by the saying, "Make me cry and I'll buy."

Sorrow is usually associated with death or divorce or illness or some other kind of loss such as loss of job, house, friendship, loss of status, etc. Sorrow may be, and often is, associated with the deprivation of love.

If illness or death is portrayed in your story, you must show the reader (editor) that deprivation of that character's love through death or serious illness is what makes our narrator suffer.

The more your narrator loves the character that is creating her sorrow, the more your narrator suffers and the stronger the story. We've just completed a circle.

- character experiences sorrow

- sorrow creates suffering

- the more your character suffers the greater chance your reader (editor) will cry

- if your reader (editor) cries you are sure of a sale!

A story in *True Romance* offered a student nurse as the narrator. She makes a serious error in the operating room during surgery on a seven year old boy. Although our narrator corrects her error in time she blames herself when Tony takes a turn for the worse. She begins spending almost all her free time with Tony. Thus we see how Tony's suffering affects the love life between our narrator and her fiancé. So we have the formula of sorrow, plus suffering, plus deprivation of love, in a story that brought many a tear stained letter to the editor.

We writers delight in those tear stained letters even if they've been sent electronically. The more "fan" mail your story receives, the higher your credit goes with Ms Editor.

ANGER AND HATE

These two emotions usually work together. We can hardly have one without the other. Hatred always drags conflict in its wake.

Anger in your dialogue, brings out the hatred and both anger and hatred appear in varying degrees. They can be spelled out or implied. For example: a mother-in-law talking to a daughter-in-law may say, "As always, you look lovely," yet by the author's implications (words, thoughts or actions) the reader knows that each woman hates the other woman's guts. This is emotion by implication

Anger is best spelled out in dialogue. If you want characters fighting mad, pour the anger on. Have the characters fighting mad through their words and their actions and their thoughts. Don't be afraid of anger.

I tell you this because most Americans, especially women, are cautioned by their parents to repress both hatred and anger. According to my mother the worst things my brother and I could say when we were children were the words, "Shut up!" which expresses anger or "I hate (insert name)!" which expresses hatred. That teaching continues to lurk in my adult life.

I can remember saying, "Shut Up!" only once when a friend who had been a guest in my house for a week kept harping at me all day about something over which I had no control. So far as I was concerned, that shouted *shut up* ripped our friendship to shreds.

I don't think I've ever said, "I hate _____" using a person as a target.

Maybe Mom didn't do me any favor by stressing such training.

Now I'm telling you to forget your good little girl or boy training. Jump right in. Get mad. Express your hatred... on paper anyway. Readers (editors) *love* anger and hate. Blow the explosive anger and hatred all out, up, down, or sideways on your page.

JOY

Readers love to cry but they also want some happiness in their reading. We writers need to attempt to place an element of joy in each story. If you can't insert happiness into the body of the story attempt to remember some past pleasure within a flashback. Have your narrator happy at some phase of her life, whether it's sex, a birthday party or just a moment of gentle contentment from watching children playing in the park.

If your narrator enjoys something, have her say so. Your reader will enjoy it also, especially if you've filled your story with conflict and hatred and anger and sorrow.

Be generous. Give her a little joy in the morning, can't you?

HOPE

Our readers experience almost all the problems we write about. They can't pay their bills. Their parents don't care about them (or vice versa). Their sons are sick. Their husbands neglect them. Their daughters are pregnant. Their other children are on drugs, and on and on. But even with all the unpleasantness in their lives they want to be able to *hope* their lives could change.

What we do with our work is give our readers hope and reassurance, by the end of the story, that there really is something better to look forward to in this world.

This is what a confession is about, assuring your readers that things will get better, despite all their real-life problems. Sometimes *you,* Mr. or Ms. Writer, can give your reader the agency that will make their lives better. We hold power in our hands.

CHAPTER 8: AMATEURS CHAT – WRITERS WRITE

Writers who view themselves as professional writers, although in some cases, not as yet published writers, should pride themselves on their use of their writing time. This applies particularly to confessions writers. We have no excuses for not working since we know how to find ideas, we have two formulas to follow (see Chapter 4) and we are expressing the drive to be published. We know our confession magazines want our stories. So the whole publishing success thing lands upon our own shoulders. All we have to do is write and submit those full-of-emotion stories.

We confessions writers have to be strict with ourselves. It's easy to dream of being published writers, but if we dream confessions while adhering to the rules, our dreams will come true. Slowly, that's true, because only *True Confessions* will answer an e-query and take an e-submission. The other *Trues* will eventually buy our stories if they fit their book's formats but they will not be swift in doing so. In the meantime, we should be unceasingly planning, outlining and writing new stories. I'm taking it for granted that all of us can write complete sentences in English.

Maybe it's too easy. We all love to sit around feeling righteous about being writers but we let ourselves become distracted. Check the items below to see which is your favorite distraction, which of these activities is your really important timewaster. And be honest with yourself. One or two or more of these timewasters could be the obstacles that keep you from being a published confessions storywriter.

TELEVISION

I know one writer who watches TV all day, every day while writing and selling book after book. More than 45 novels at last count. But hey, she's the exception. And she shall remain nameless. Never mind her. We confessions writers can send for transcripts of Oprah's or Dr. Phil's shows if we think they might give us ideas for stories but that is about it. We need to keep the television off during the day if that's when we schedule our writing time... or off at night, if we are working for wages in the daytime and writing at night.

TELEPHONE

Some of us can't let a telephone ring without answering. We should cultivate the art of ignoring that seductive ring. Let it go onto your message machine unless it is an editor calling. Then you cut in and talk. Otherwise we should use the telephone for what it is...a personal convenience. Keep away from chitchat to friends and relatives in your free time, that is, time not dedicated to writing. Call local people you need to talk to from the telephone at your wage-earning job.

ELECTRONIC COMMUNICATION

I never thought I would become a slave to my computer. I was totally ignorant of the machine and half afraid of it when I switched from the typewriter. A few years ago I learned about email. I knew I had to learn the electronic stuff but I always tried to put it off until the end of the day. Now it is an established habit for me to go to the email messages just before I head to bed. As I've timed myself, I've realized that I sometimes spend an hour or more at the email, reading, answering and sending original stuff. As I get more practiced I spend more time, so let me warn you... the electronic baby can eat your time quite ably. Use it for writing but forget about jokes, sending notes, surfing the web, instant email, and all the stuff that can become so tempting and time consuming. Be careful. This alley is full of dead careers even though those so-called writers are punching away at the keys.

ERRANDS

We're eaten up with this one… and we're always able to justify the time spent… had to go to Office Depot, the post office, the library… etc., etc. And while we're out we need to stop by the bank… and on and on. Mea Culpa. I reluctantly do this stuff all the time and every time I have to rush to the bookstore I'm consumed with guilt. I should be home with my computer. Writing.

One of the best answers I've found is: *don't dress*! If you're in your underwear or your nightgown, you can't make so many trips, although you can make some. I used to throw a caftan over my nightgown and drive Ms Hazel to Sunday School. (Someone else brought her home.)

Never accept luncheon dates is another ploy that helps me. I wait to hear your bits of wisdom on curing this career cancer.

FRIENDS, RELATIVES AND NEIGHBORS

"You're at home all day, aren't you dear?" Could you look after the kids for a few hours, take in our deliveries, eat lunch with me, iron my shirt, take the girl scout cookies to the people in the neighborhood and on and on it goes. Become well acquainted with the word "*NO*." Stick to your guns; friends. Family and neighbors can learn!

READING

We are writers so we like nothing so much as reading. Oh, my soul, yes. We must read, of course, to keep up with the field in which we write, but this is the special temptation that consumes my time. Reading a book every day is simply self-indulgent. I do it. I admit to addiction. Help. Help. I say to other writers, "Be stern with yourself. Say to yourself, "Only about twelve percent of my writing time can be spent reading materials which are directly related to my writing project. No more!"

Yes, I say this, but I ignore my own good advice entirely. Don't fall into this hole which I've allowed to consume me. This is one of those rules where you must do as I say, not as I do.

RESEARCH

We writers love to get lost in the library. It seems so writerly to get oneself lost in the stacks. Here's my advice. Write your confessions story, beginning to end, then go directly to the children's section of the library and get the one or two facts that seem important to fill the holes in your story. This is more a trap for nonfiction writers but confessions writers can get caught up in research as well.

ARRANGING YOUR OFFICE

This is not my problem so, of course, I have little sympathy for you folks who spend hours and days, "getting things in order." True, we should be able to find things in our files and we should be able to move through the room without hindrance, but filing and record keeping can be saved to be done at a particular time… say, once a week (month?) after the hours we've committed to writing our confessions.

EATING, SMOKING POT, DRINKING, SEEKING SEX, DRUGGING OUT, RUNNING MORE THAN EIGHT MILES A DAY, OR ANY OTHER STUPID HABIT YOU'VE PICKED UP ALONG THE WAY

Two of these habits have been dogging me for years. (I'll let you guess which two.) We do eventually have to put down that coffee cup and get to work if we're going to get any work done.

WAITING FOR THE MUSE TO DESCEND UPON YOUR HEAD

This is a bit of silliness reserved for amateurs. We confessions writers can't pay one moment of attention to this nonsense.

BEING BLOCKED

More nonsense. We real confessions writers have much too much mental balance to loll around on this couch. Rewriting yesterday's work is all the jump-start we need to get on to writing today's stuff. We've all surely heard the phrase, "Just do it!"

CHAPTER 9: SET GOALS

I can tell you how to sell to the confessions but you're the one who has to actually do the work, then sell it. Never mind anything I have said or will say to you, there are only five things you can do to make yourself into a published confessions writer. Those five things are as follows:

1. Decide you want to be writer of confessions stories

2. Choose a place to write

3. Choose a time to write

4. Write to the needs of the market

5. Submit what you have written

Easy? Yes and no. Writing is never easy, but making up your mind, setting goals and working toward those achievements is terribly difficult for some people. Can you do the five things listed above? Well, if you answered *yes*, then, you can be a confessions storywriter but nothing can happen until you commit, write and submit.

EYES ON THE PRIZE

What is the prize? Money, of course, but with no byline you can still experience a ton of satisfaction when you see your very own stories printed in a national magazine. The satisfaction comes from seeing the stories but also from the knowledge that you set yourself a goal and then achieved that goal through work, study and determination. Goal setting may be the very best thing you can do for yourself when you enter the world of the *Trues*.

One of my friends, Jackie King, in Tulsa, took classes in confessions writing with two different teachers. (Yes, I was one of them!) and told herself she could do that (write and sell confessions) and she did, a couple of times but she got married, had three kids to raise and worked at a fulltime, very demanding job so she worked at writing when she had time and the writing, even though she wasn't selling, improved year after year. She came to some of my classes to try to hone her craft and it all turned out pretty well. She took early retirement and one of the goals she had staked out for herself in her new job... being a fulltime writer, was the sale of a confession story each and every month, even though she was working on a couple of novels and several short stories for women's magazines that don't offer confessions. How is she doing? Very well.

Jackie has sold a confession every month since she took on the job of fulltime writing. Some months she has sold two confessions. Thirty stories so far have been published and more to come for which she has signed contracts. Now she is also writing books.

How did she do that you may very well ask? The answer is, she set a goal, did her daily stint and now, she is a working, selling writer. The husband, the kids and the cat are all gone from her house now, one way or another, so she is making great strides down her chosen path. For purposes of this book I asked her what she had received from confessions this month. (Please, don't you do that. It is terribly rude to ask people what they are being paid, but for your benefit I allowed myself to be rude this one time.) "$440.00." she answered me. Um hmm. I think we'd all love to be able to say that our writing brought us that amount or any other amount of money each month. What a thrill for a beginning writer!

I asked her to explain exactly how she, a new writer, went about making herself into this paragon of accomplished goals. Would she please lay out her daily schedule so we could follow in her footsteps? "Surely," she said and here is what she told me:

"First I shower and put on my makeup. Then I have a bowl of cereal and my coffee. After that I take my exercises or walk in the mall. Back home I go straight to my computer and do my five confession pages. If the five pages pour out I may go on and do as many more pages as come forth easily, but I never stop until I've done my five pages, no matter how long it takes. After lunch I work on other projects (unless I'm still trying for my five confession pages) except for the two afternoons a week when I do marketing work."

See? King made a plan, set a goal, and she sticks to her plan and she has had great success working toward her goal. I am especially struck by the makeup bit. I asked about it.

"I'm going to work," she told me, "All the years I worked in an office I showered, made up my face, dressed, ate and went to work. I'm still doing that. The makeup signifies 'workday' to my psyche, I suppose. I'm just taking 25 steps to my office rather than driving five miles to work. I really love my life now. I'm doing something I love"

I was so proud to see Jackie meet her goals. You can do the same thing Jackie King did.

YOUR ABILITIES AS A WRITER

One of the things that many writers have found to help them become as successful as Jackie has been so far, requires a bit of thought about what you really want. Along with the long-term plans you need to be honing your craft, even though you may be limited to one, two, three, or four hours per day for your writing. You need to be taking classes, reading books about writing, studying confessions magazines, going to conferences and most importantly, you need to be writing, writing, writing.

A big part of your goal setting may devolve onto 3x5 cards. I'm talking about affirmations. Written affirmations require that you set down goals for now and on into the future.

Let's look at five years from today. Always write your affirmations in the positive form. State your goal for where you wish to be as a writer in five years. Write whatever you wish on scratch paper then boil the whole thing down to one good sentence. Put the final positive version on your card. Put your card in a place where you will see it each day. I have often used the medicine chest mirror. I know I'm going to brush my teeth so I know I will be in front of that particular place two or three times a day, maybe more.

For a few days you will read the card consciously. Then you will have to force yourself to read it, then you will forget to read it, and then you'll forget that the card is there at all. But even though you are no longer attentive to your five year goal, a part of you is quite aware of the card and reading your affirmation each and every time you step in front of the medicine chest. What part? It's your subconscious, darling. Your subconscious believes you meant what you said on your card and your subconscious is reading and pushing you along the road to do and be what you've put out on your mirror via your affirmation cards.

Of course, you were realistic. Make sure your goals are not too far in the future. Make sure your goals are set by you and not by someone else. Make sure your goal is reasonable. A million dollars for confessions stories over five years is not reasonable.

Make your goal tangible and dependant upon your own efforts alone. You have to train for your goal, go to class, read, work with a critique group, pay attention to the stories around you, enter contests, etc. There are a number of things you can do to help yourself reach your goal. All those things are good but the main thing you must do is_____. (Did you fill in the blank with the word, "write?")

Make another card for your immediate future, for this year. You need to think, scribble ideas, then make a clear copy which sets your priorities and delineates what you are longing to have.

Close your eyes when you begin to plan for the immediate future and for the more distant future of five years. While your eyes are closed visualize yourself accepting an award for your confession story or article. Visualize yourself receiving an editor's acceptance by mail, telephone or email. Visualize yourself signing a contract. Visualize yourself making a copy of your first check to hang on your office wall. Visualize yourself cashing that check.

Dreams, combined with concrete plans, mixed into hard work, will make you into a successful confessions writer. Call me at

918-834-6365 or tell me by email, peggy@PeggyFielding .com or write me a letter, P.O. Box 50347, Tulsa, OK 74150 when you make your first sale. I will be as thrilled as you will be, I promise you. Your husband, lover, friend, brother, mother or sister will be happy but not a one of those folks will completely understand what a thrill this sale is. I will know exactly what you are feeling and I will be proud of you.

Remember, goals have to do with writing, marketing, contests, writing groups or clubs, prizes and other writers. You can make your affirmation cards deal with anyone of those things which are important to you as a writer.

You can also check up on me. Go to my website www.peggyfielding.com and subscribe free to my newsletter. Each month I will confess and tell on myself and sometimes I will talk about you.

SPELLING AND OTHER STUFF COUNTS

By the way, your fifth grade teacher was right. Neatness counts. Spelling does too. Beautiful, correctly spelled manuscripts will help take you to your goals.

CHAPTER 10: DRAW A CONFESSION

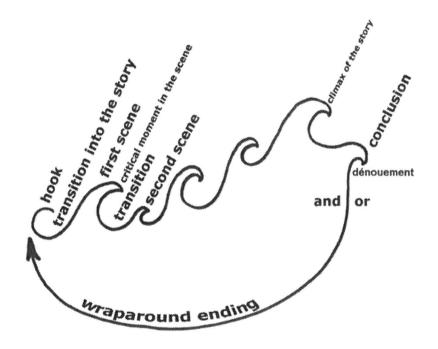

Study the drawing above. This is a chart (a picture?) of a successful confessions story.

You'll open with a hook. Your first sentence or two should grab the reader's attention. By the end of the first paragraph or, at most, by the end of the second paragraph, your reader (editor) should have a good idea as to what problem your narrator is facing and the reader should also have gained at least a tiny clue as to how our viewpoint character is planning to solve her problem.

The hook sentence or paragraph should be fairly short and it should present some startling, pithy, sad, amusing, frightening, or strong action information. The hook doesn't have to be blood or train crashes or that kind of startling or active sentence. It can he something from the heart, soul, mind, or gut of our narrator, something that grabs the reader's attention.

Here are some examples of first lines or hooks which I'm just jotting onto the page with no real story in mind. Writers who have stories in mind can come up with *much better hooks, I'm sure.*

I don't think John loves me anymore.

The teacher's words still rang in my mind.

Sometimes God answers my prayers with the words, "No Karen."

"Your Mother's moving in with us?"

My stepfather died yesterday and, I must admit, I was glad of it.

The hook sentences, then one or two hook paragraphs lead naturally into a sentence or phrase of transition in preparation for the first scene, which reveals a great deal about why our narrator is concerned with a particular problem.

Here are some transitions into first scenes... to follow the hooks above. I'm sure you can come up with better transitions for your stories. Transitions might be called pathways, gateways or passages of words that move readers into the next scene.

Later he asked me to stay home.

He buttoned his coat without a word, then left the classroom.

I try to do what I think God wants me to do.

At the window in the guestroom I stared out without seeing a thing.

```
It started when I was ten.
```

Now you've moved fully into your first scene. This wave starts higher than the second scene because this wave imparts such important information; really the crux of what is worrying our narrator.

As is true in each of the three or four following scenes, there is a climactic moment in each wave (scene) which is symbolized by the point of the wave. That climactic moment for the scene can be a bit of information, a realization or a decision on the part of our narrator or simply a declaration or action on the part of our heroine.

Once the climactic moment is reached in each scene, there is a transition by word, phrase, sentence or paragraph into the next scene. The transitional words are symbolized by the troughs between the waves. This change of scene does not infer physical movement into a different setting, although that can be what you use. Often the scene change is signaled by new thought, dialogue, or action on the part of our narrator… and so it goes through each scene until you reach the largest wave, the most climactic scene of the whole story.

The last or climactic scene, is the scene in the story where your narrator chooses to do the right thing at last and we see her doing that.

This climactic scene clears the way for the story conclusion which offers a tiny crisis moment of its own, followed by the dénouement. (day-new-mah).

The dénouement is a fancy French word that writers have adopted. It is the last bottom of the wave in our drawing and instead of being called a transition, we call it the dénouement, which means, "How it all turned out," and you can cover that in a few words or a sentence or a paragraph or two. Some examples of dénouement material to go with the previous examples are as follows:

```
I need to learn to control my
imagination, especially on dreary days.
```

It's good to know that there are real organizations of real people who can help me face building a new routine with Junior.

I've learned to trust God to steer me in the right direction.

Now I get to sleep half an hour later since Jim's Mother has taken over the breakfast chores.

My sense of relief allowed the weight I'd been carrying on my shoulders for years to slide completely away and disappear.

FINISHING UP

Now, after the dénouement sentence(s), if you want to, you may take a phrase, sentence or paragraph to point back to the hook in some way. Editors like this neat wraparound style if you can manage it. Some examples following our previous sentence examples:

The starry sky reflected the wonder of John's declaration.

"Mom, I really like school now," Junior's parting words made me smile all the way to work.

"Thank you, Lord." was my only comment.

Pancakes in the morning can make up for a whole bushel of sacrifices.

I helped my Mother stand and we both looked into a sunny future.

See?

If you follow a few basic guidelines and pattern after the wave drawing, selling to the confessions should be only a matter of time and practice.

Keep in mind the things you'll need to succeed, which are:

- A sympathetic narrator, first person viewpoint, the right tone (intimate, natural, peppered with convincing dialogue and good monologue which is your heroine's narration from front to back.) Remember that introspection is a great way to promote reader sympathy.

- Use a flashback only if it deepens our understanding of the narrator's problem. Keep it short if you must use a flashback.

- Using the drawing as your guide, strive for texture and hominess. Details are important. If a child is sick, what is his illness? Is the family dog a mutt from the pound? In each wave try to include friends, family, neighborhood, hopes, fears, job, house, church, etc.

REVIEW

In your stories your narrator must act upon and solve whatever problem is facing her. Readers feel cheated with a "then I realized" ending. Take your reader through the hoops that your narrator must go through in order to find her moment of truth.

Here is a review of the ten basic guidelines for writing and selling confessions, and they are:

1. Build a sympathetic narrator

2. Show the first person viewpoint

3. Use a confessions story tone

4. Present flashbacks (or not!)

5. Imbed texture and hominess

6. Open with a great hook

7. Demonstrate only one problem

8. Put in plenty of drama and conflict

9. Have your narrator act to solve her own problem

10. Try to bring your story full circle

Let the waves take you and your story as far as it needs to go.

IF I COULD JUST SPELL I COULD
PROBABLY WRITE CONFESSIONS

CHAPTER 11: DIALOGUE FRONT TO BACK, TOP TO BOTTOM

The real difference in our kind of short story and other types of short stories is in the voice. Our voice is first person. "I." tells the whole story, all from her point of view.

YOUR STORY IS A CONVERSATION

Each of our stories (at least most of them) is a conversation between your narrator and her friend, who just happens to be a reader. She can be an editor or the person who buys your magazine. She is able to converse with you and to hear your story. Mentally, our reader is comparing her own problems to the problem talked about by your heroine in her story. You're writing various kinds of dialogue, front to back, top to bottom.

You need to try to get the story from the horse's mouth. If you are writing about rape perhaps you'll want to volunteer for rape counseling work. My word, working for a rape counseling center, what a great way for a writer to get a million ideas for stories!

However, if you don't want to take on such a responsibility, you can get ideas for future stories by listening, reading, observing TV, looking at columns in magazines such as *The Ladies Home Journal* and *The Enquirer* which offer "true" stories that can be fictionalized. You can watch soaps or rent old movies, observe your friends and foes. How about "Dear Abby" and/or old columns by Ann Landers? Pay attention at the supermarket check out counters and other places of work. What are those pink collar workers talking about?

SET THE TONE OF THE STORY

Drama and conflict set the tone of your story. The conversational style also helps maintain the expected intimate tone of a confessions story.

Get into, inside of, the character you've chosen as spokesperson. Once you've become your character you then *tell* on yourself. That is what confessing is all about. You're sharing your innermost thoughts with a trusted friend.

Let the natural flow of the "I" viewpoint display your narrator's secrets, prejudices and heartaches. Your thoughts are displayed through her own special vocabulary, her occupational jargon, her sensory impressions and her pain and suffering or her joy. Her character is revealed through her monologues, her inner dialogue, as well as in the spoken dialogue that shows up between quotation marks.

My Tulsa writing students (other than those in the confessions classes) are going to be shocked at my next bit of advice. I most often say to them, "Please don't use italics." However, for our stories you will sometimes use italics. You show italics by underlining even though you have italic print on your machine. Editors and typesetters are used to the underlining as the signal for italics, so do it that way.

When the going gets especially tough for your narrator you will use monologue and dialogue, of course, but you may also wish to lay out a little *inner* dialogue, which is shown with underlining in your manuscript. This touch of *inner dialogue* puts your narrator on a direct line to your reader. *I'm like any other mother,* she pleads with her reader, *Try to understand why I did this to my child.* And we readers do try to understand why she did what she did.

The tiny nuggets of italics must not be overdone but these tiny bits and pieces come through your story like a hand reaching out of the page to grasp the shoulder of your reader. Put a little of yourself into your narrator, but let each story heroine follow her own dreams, experience her own pain, and let her speak in her own unique way.

MAKE YOURSELF INTO A PROFESSIONAL

Well, how do I do that, Peggy? One thing you can do is read, read, read. Buy confessions and read them. In fact, I think subscriptions to several of the confessions magazines would be quite professional of you. Go to the area where black confessions are sold and buy some of them as well. You may find you'd like to write for that market as well as for the white confessions. (The illustrations and the rule about one sex scene per story, are what make the magazines one or the other.)

Do research. Pay attention to what problems you, your friends and others are facing. Get lists of helpful organizations and institutions. Call hot lines and find their e-equivalents online at your computer.

Keep files of what you hear, see or think you can write about.

Write every day, even if only for an hour. This is your art but it is also your business so you need to practice your art in a businesslike manner.

Learn to submit your work in the way each magazine wants to see it. Send finished stories to the magazines as hard copy, enclose a disc and forget about them, except within your records, for six to eight months. Yes, it sometimes takes that long, but do keep track of submission dates and check back when necessary, by mail, email, or telephone. These stories are your children and you want to know at all times what is happening to them.

When a story is rejected, look it over to see what needs to be done for the appearance of the manuscript, then after the clean-up, get that rejected story off to the next magazine on your list of confessions to which you plan to submit. Never, ever, give up! Rewriting, if necessary, is not a sin, it is just a part of being professional.

TRY CHARACTER SKETCHES

Especially at the beginning of your confessions career, you may want to do character sketches for at least your narrator. You may also want to lay out sketches for your secondary characters.

I'm not telling you to learn to draw, although there is nothing wrong with cutting out pictures that look like the person you've envisioned. Our art is not with paint on paper. Our art uses words on paper so we make out sheets that tell a great deal about our main characters. We call these "character sketches."

Physical characteristics are not so important as other characteristics. This is for yourself so don't resent the effort. What is her problem for this story? What is her place in her family? What is her job? What is her education? What are her marital arrangements? What is her secret? What is her weakness? What is her age? Answer these and any other questions which seem important to your story.

Try to lay out, whether one or two pages, as much as you can about your characters. You'll just be making your job easier for yourself.

CONFESSIONS CAN BE WRITTEN BY YOUNG OR OLD, MALE OR FEMALE, FAT OR THIN, UGLY AS WELL AS BEAUTY-PAGEANT-LOVELY WRITERS.

CHAPTER 12: THE BUSINESS OF WRITING CONFESSIONS

Confessions writing is an art but it's also a business if you're serious about wanting to be a published writer. Unless you happen to have an assistant to attend to your business affairs, you're elected to that post. Having your spouse or parent or friend take care of business for you is not a good idea. It's much better to involve yourself in your own writing business so you know what is going on in your career.

No one can expect you to "write" more than three or four hours per day. By writing we're talking about freshly pouring out our confessions stories onto paper. That leaves four or five hours for other business if you're working full time as a writer: i.e. 8 hours a day.

However many hours you've carved out for writing, half of your carved-out time will be business, such as telephoning, interviewing, record keeping, making the office livable, reading and a number of other chores which must be accomplished in a business day. If you can only work at writing for two hours a day, half of that time (1 hour) will be used for writing and l hour will be used for attending to business chores.

KEEPING RECORDS

Much of my writing record keeping has been done on 3x5 cards or spiral notebooks. And yes, I know most people can now keep records on a computer. I am computer impaired so I cling to my cards and notebooks and you may do that as well if you wish.

There are several important items that you must write down for your own peace of mind and for the government's peace of mind, as well.

One important item is your sales list. You'll keep all your sales on this list for each year, not just your confessions, but each category will have its own category listing, such as: Nonfiction

Books, Novels, Articles, Confessions, Poetry, Plays, etc. Keep the list for yourself, at first. Later you'll use a less detailed version of the list as a selling tool to be sent to potential publishers or agents whom you wish to snare. Write the name of the piece and when and where it sold. For your editor or agent put no amounts or other info, please. Editors don't need to know how much you received for your materials. You don't know what the editor's weekly paychecks display, do you?

Your own list will look something like this:

SALES 200- to 200-

ARTICLES
Date -We Owe It To Our Kids – PTA News $15.00 Asked for
    more articles of this type
Date – Q telephone Gone With The Wind – Tulsa Kids $45.00

CONFESSIONS
Date – I Had Sex With An Old Man – True Confessions R
    Date True Story $150.00
Date – I'm In Love With My Stepson – True Romance
    $165.00
Date – Sultry Sex With Strangers: And It's My Husband's
    Fault – True Confessions $220.00
Date – I Need a Man For Valentines Day – True Confessions
    $220.00 Editor wants an inspirational set in the Easter
    season
Date – I Traded My Body For A House – True Love $180.00

ESSAYS
Date – Completely Out of Range – Grit $50.00. Wants more
Date – Gone With The Wind – Sapulpa Herald - $10.00

NONFICTION BOOKS
Date – Salesmanager's Guide – Simon & Schuster $8000.00
    in 3 payments

Date – Writing And Selling Magazine Articles –
    AWOC.COM no advance, royalties paid monthly

NOVELS

Date – (reissue) Paradise Found –Zebra $3000.00 advance
    royalties paid twice yearly
Date – Sally – Hard Shell Word Factory - No advance,
    royalties paid twice yearly. Wants a regency
Date – A Stadium Kind of Love –AWOC.com – No advance
    royalties paid monthly

POETRY

Date – Harpooned Heart – Nimrod -3 copies
Date – Smiling Sunday – Mature Living $10.00

…AND SO ON AS YOUR SALES EXPAND.

Titles cannot be copyrighted. Your publisher will attend to copyrights for everything else. Getting the copyright is not your business unless you are self publishing and, of course, you won't be self-publishing your confessions.

With your private submissions record you are keeping the history of each piece you write. Q stands for Query. This record also gives you info about what editors liked and what they want for the future, perhaps.

For your own records you need to keep a copy of each story, where it sold, editor comments, and how much and when you were paid. Hard copies in file cabinets and/or bookcases work best for me but you can do this electronically I suppose as well, if you have plenty of space within your computer memory for keeping all those confessions and notes about them.

See Chapter 16 for some electronic methods for record keeping but, for Heaven's Sake, don't ask me! I know less than nothing about computers.

"This is a *personal* computer ma'am. You confess your problems to it and it comes up with a story."

TICKLER/RETIRED

This special file is your memory-reminder file. Magazines usually want your stories six to eight months ahead of actual publication date, so a tickler file can remind you when it is time to start work on that Valentine or Easter or Christmas confession.

This file (in my notebook, your computer) also holds retired stuff. I put returned confessions here because I may be unable to sell this story this month or year but perhaps three years from now that retired confession can be plumped up, fluffed out, and sent out again.

Never throw any of your work away! Sometimes those puppies will hunt in another season. Never give up!

EXPENSE/MILEAGE FILE/ACCOUNTANT

Your other files deal with money: i.e. expenses and receipts. I use an expense record book from Office Depot. You may want to use your computer. This is for your own benefit but also for the benefit of the Government. The IRS may ask to see your financial files and you must be ready to produce them upon demand.

A notebook for mileage should be kept in your car. All miles driven to research or interview or to take care of other writer business, should be logged. Trips to conferences or seminars must also be noted. Check to see what the current government mileage rate is per mile so you can take these miles off your income tax.

Obtain a bookkeeper or an accountant who can be trained to watch over your income tax and SS monies. You will probably have to be the one who does the training unless you know a writer who is willing to share the name of her knowledgeable accountant. These writer-trained accountants are as treasured as the "little dressmaker" once was to fashionable women of society. Really trainable, understanding, patient number-crunchers are hard to come by. Of course, you or your spouse can do the reporting but if you're at all like me, you don't want to deal with numbers. I say, let someone else do the IRS, SS stuff, someone who enjoys doing that sort of work. I'll be writing to pay his or her fee.

If you're reporting to Washington D.C; as a full time writer you need to fill out forms for the IRS four times a year. If you're working at other jobs or if you're combining your report with your spouse's income tax return, you can probably do the once a year thing

ITEMS WHICH CAN BE WRITTEN OFF YOUR INCOME TAX

Home Office: The IRS can be a bit sticky about this so be sure you can prove that the space is used for your writing work only. No baby cribs, no ironing boards, no beds, no clothing storage, etc. An outside entrance to the space helps but an inside entrance is okay if your furnishings demonstrate that serious writing work goes on in that area.

Some of the things which are acceptable in a home office: Radio, TV, VCR, record player, CD, Tape recorder – Most writers like music to write by. Some use talk shows on TV for market research materials. Some just like the sound of company. Any or all of these items are write-offs. You can also write off other items such as your desk, chairs, file cabinets, typewriters, computers, printer, copy machine, shredder, table, etc, or any other "office" equipment.

OTHER WRITE-OFFS

- All postage or shipping costs

- All books, magazines or newspapers, purchased individually or through subscription. All library fees or book rental prices. Everything you read is "market research," you know.

- All classes or conferences about writing.

- All classes that help with your writing, such as computer classes, grammar classes, literature classes, photography classes, and so on.

- All writing club memberships (local, state and/or national groups)

Hurrah! I can take off the cost of all my subscriptions when I do my taxes

- Any machines or furniture for use in your writing space, including TV and VCR if you use them for research or for company while writing. Wall décor and decorating costs may also be taken off.

- The telephone, if it is exclusive to your office or is listed as a 'business' telephone may be written off.

- Postage or P.O. Box rental.

- All office supplies. Ink, staples, glue, paper, envelopes, scotch tape, pens and pencils, discs, paper clips.

- Half of all your 'entertainment,' such as food, call-girls, feeding an editor, or whatever meal or show you might use to help you to interview a subject or cement your relationship with the publishing powers that be.

CHAPTER 13: WHAT EDITORS WANT NOW

Editors want you to keep your story ordinary and believable, but written with a fresh flair. Neither editors nor confessions readers want to read about terrible people who have horrible things happening to them. They want to read about a normal person who has a problem and who has made a wrong choice or two while trying to solve her problem.

Reader identity is very important. Make your narrator a person with a blue collar (or pink collar) background in a small, neat house or apartment with a man who works at a nonprofessional job and you can't go far wrong.

EMOTION, EMOTION, EMOTION

Readers (editors) really want to see lots of agonizing and hand wringing. A middle class, stiff-upper-lip demeanor, just doesn't cut it here. Let's have a little shouting, crying, and painful heartache in most stories. You'll find a bit of this emotional stuff even in the lighthearted, funny confessions. Of course, joy and laughter are emotions also.

Well, Peggy, what are editors looking for right now? This very moment?

Here is what I've learned. Editors are seeking present day stories of the types listed below. You have long realized, no doubt, that confessions are not just a morass of sex as your grandmother imagined. Today's confession tells of one woman's problem and how she solves it. Set your problem in one of the following areas and your editor will greet you with glad cries.

Inspirational stories: These don't have to touch on religion, certainly they are not sermons. God, prayer, religious strength, family, church habits, counseling, etc. figure here. A little supernatural help such as angels, can't hurt. The editor at *True*

Confessions told me straight to my face that she was avid for inspirational stories.

Small town stories: Many literary or commercial short stories are set in New York City, Hollywood, San Francisco, Dallas or perhaps Chicago. Our readers either live in small towns or come from families in small towns. There is an unassuaged longing for small town stories in the American psyche. Go visit your cousin in Poteau, Oklahoma or Poulsbo, Washington if you've never lived in a small town. Get the feel of such a place.

Teen Stories: *True Confessions* and *True Story* are both searching for stories told from the teen viewpoint, fourteen to eighteen year olds. All you have to do is remember that your teenage customs, favorite places and activities have changed somewhat. No one goes to a soda fountain or to a "sock hop" anymore except under exceptional circumstances. Watch and listen to your kids but leave out their slang or bywords. Those things change constantly and we can't keep abreast.

Cinderella stories: As in "I turned my life around and so can you." We're not talking about working as a chamber maid in a hotel then accidentally marrying a rich man as J. Lo did, but we can write of a fat girl who loses weight or learns to love herself as she is and appeals to a man who also loves her. A farm girl can end up marrying a plumber and they can start their own business. These stories lean hard on the real efforts of our narrator and her significant other. No fairy godmothers.

Older woman, younger man: Handled well, editors love this. You might go down the road of tall woman, short male, etc. Any out-of-the–norm combination might make a readable story.

Adoption and/or infertility: Remember our readers think a family of father, mother, two kids and a dog is the ultimate good in life. Even single women settle for spinisterhood plus mother-hood as a way of being fulfilled. Medical stories of all sorts, if handled with delicacy, really sell. Infertility is high on our list of problems to write about.

Child in jeopardy: Wow! This hits all the sensitive sore spots in our reading audience. We American women love, protect and value children, especially our own, but we also feel for all children who are suffering, even children who do not belong to us. This is a rich field for our writing. Our child in jeopardy should probably live in the U.S.A. or be from the U.S.A. or be born to an American woman originally.

Animal stories: The animals can be the main thrust of the story or they can appear in our stories accompanying our narrator in some way. Dogs are now outnumbering cats in American households for the first time in years.

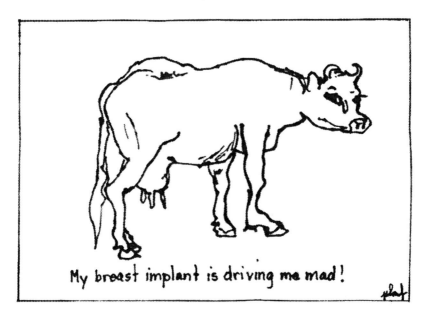

My breast implant is driving me mad!

Holiday or special day stories: Write something fresh for Christmas and the editor will kiss your toes. These stories must be in to your editor 6 to 8 months before the special day. Holidays are both official, such as Christmas and unofficial, such as Groundhog day. Special times of the year are June for brides and end of school, school vacations, special local celebrations such as autumn leaf tours, etc. Look for fresh points of view.

THE THREE D's

Death, disease and deprivation of love, especially divorce, have always been the basis for many of the problems of our narrators. Naturally, our narrator's death is not what we write about. We write about how the death of someone else affects her and her life. Disease can affect her and our readers. And divorce is just awful. Our readers love to read about these problems and how our narrators overcome them.

Census figures tell us that nowadays, half our married population will divorce sooner or later, causing all kind of problems for both men and women. What is bad for them is good for us as writers! We can use their pain.

Deprivation of love is the spine of many a confession story. Everyone wants to be loved, our story characters most of all. This problem, deprivation of love, appears in about 60 percent of the stories sold to confession magazines.

Now deprivation of love isn't always the deprivation of sexual love. You did know that, didn't you? Sometimes it is loss of parental love, loss of a child's love, or even the loss of friendship.

If we can deprive our girl of love in some way we can be sure of a sale if we follow the confessions formula.

CHAPTER 14: AND WHAT THEY DON'T WANT

There are several "don'ts" for confessions storywriters. Most confession stories that are rejected are sent back to us not because of bad writing but because of what we writers do to our stories. There are a number of things that may cause your story to be returned to you. Let's talk about them.

Here are twelve "don'ts" for confession writers. You may wish to flip back to Chapter 4 for confessions taboos just to remind yourself of subjects you may want to avoid as well.

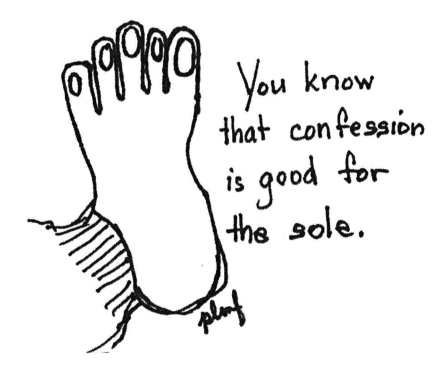

You know that confession is good for the sole.

Don't have a narrator who is unlikable or she will have no reader sympathy. Our readers can't afford psychiatrists. They are trying to help themselves. Our narrator who has a similar problem points a way for them in their lonely struggle. They feel good that she has hope but they want her to be decent. Would you want to read 5,000 words about a narrator who takes dope, fights, screams, kicks, brags, lies, or steals, without ever doing anything nice? Our girl has to be concerned about her problem. She also has to be concerned about her husband's physical and emotional health, his clothes, his job, the kids, her mother, the neighbors, their dog or cat and so on. In general, these concerns are peripheral to the main problem presented by the story but are within the province of our girl just the same.

Don't have Karen make a mistake or get into trouble without a good reason. You have to explain why she has gotten herself into this fix. Did she have an unfortunate experience as a child? Was she raised in painful poverty? Did her parents expect perfection? Was she the "ugly duckling" at school? We need to see/hear what she is thinking about and learn why she has come to this point.

Don't have long flashbacks. 300 words or fewer are best until you become a really practiced confessions writer.

Don't have too many characters. If you must have children use only one or two who are important to the plot. Actor W. C. Fields said it once when rejecting a script containing child actors, "Kids always steal the scene."

Don't have another character change drastically if the story is essentially the narrator's tale about her own change.

Don't use sex just for the sake of sex.

Don't have a narrator who neglects her children. Motherhood is looked upon with great tenderness by our readers. No matter what kind of trouble Karen is in, how many errors she has made, she must be concerned about her children or the children in her care (Aside from the story of difficulties accepting a handicapped child.) No matter how Karen suffers, she must care and love and fight for her kids.

Don't have Karen confess an incident rather than a problem to be solved. This is the number one error of rejected stories editors tell me. Teen, unmarried, is pregnant. Father of baby missing somehow. Boy next door offers to marry her. After some discussion they marry. All this story says to unmarried readers is that if you get pregnant don't worry. Someone is bound to marry you. In the above case the boy next door has solved the narrator's problem by marrying her. Karen hasn't told reader the circumstances leading up to her pregnancy and she has not changed her future outlook. She did not solve her problem herself through her own actions. The only thing that changed was her marital status.

Don't have a character change without some planting along the way. Example: Karen's friend is introduced. Friend seems sweet and charming all through the story then suddenly at the end he/she turns out to be a rotter. With no planted hint to the reader this sudden change is dismaying to the reader. The reverse is also true. Bad to suddenly good doesn't work either. Give a few hints. If the plot calls for it, keep readers guessing without giving away that character's true nature but plant a few hints. Let her kick the dog when she thinks she is unobserved. Nothing sudden. Be subtle.

Don't change the narrator's problem midstream. If Karen's problem is jealousy, keep it jealousy throughout the story, right to the last word. Don't confuse jealousy with any other problem, such as vindictiveness, or sibling rivalry... which is a form of jealousy but not jealousy, per se.

Don't introduce an incident which has nothing to do with the narrator's problem or situation. Each scene must relate to your theme (Karen's problem) and carry the story forward to her own solution.

Don't have other characters solve Karen's problem

I HAVE THIS PROBLEM, LADIES
LET ME TELL YOU MY STORY.

CHAPTER 15: NO SEX IS OKAY

Confessions stories can be sexless. Does that surprise you? Many people, including your grandmother, think all confessions are all just sex. Period.

And they would be wrong. Period.

True, there are plenty of stories dealing with lust, sex, and man-woman love but if you limit yourself to that particular subject you're missing a large and lucrative other market.

What are the sexless confessions? They can be about family, job, or medical problems. They can be about children, pets or in-laws. They can be about brushes with the law or customs of the community. They can be occult, religious, or about school happenings. In other words, confessions can be written using the same subject matter that is used by other writers in other fields.

There are certain elements that help make the sex-free story more salable. These elements can be used alone or in combination to help you sell your story.

EMOTION

If you weep into your computer while you write your story it's as good as sold. "Tearjerkers" are favorites of readers and editors.

One story called "A Child's Last Gift," told of a young mother who withdrew from life after her son was killed in an automobile accident. The child's dog, who survived the accident, eventually becomes the channel through which the mother is able to accept and adjust to the loss of her son and begin living again with hope.

Another story called "My Special Gift to Grandma" was about a young woman who "adopts" an elderly nursing home patient. Their relationship developed and the ideas they shared enriched both their lives. The story was set in the Christmas season.

HELP FOR THE READER

If a story can offer practical suggestions for overcoming a problem, readers are grateful and your story is sold.

A story called, "I Was Blamed For My Baby's Death" explored the subject of Sudden Infant Death Syndrome (SIDS) Thorough research will be required to get the medical facts right in such a story. This story emphasized ways to deal with the guilt that is such a common parental reaction to such tragedy. The name and address of a national organization for parents who have lost a child to SIDS was embedded in the story so readers could learn where to write or call or search the web for help.

In such a story, be sure that any self-help techniques you suggest are medically and/or psychologically sound.

ESCAPE FROM THE HUMDRUM

The occult or religious-miraculous story may take readers outside themselves, away from their ordinary days.

In a story I wrote for *True Story* called , "She Tried To Steal My Life," my narrator's cousin came to stay with our girl after her parents death. The visiting cousin used occult means to try to steal our girl's life and lifestyle, including our girl's boyfriend. Our girl's spiritual strength helped her get away from the predatory cousin and cousin dies in a fire she herself set to kill our heroine.

In another story, "Premonition of Disaster," a young mother is going to chaperone a field trip for her daughter's class. As they board the bus, the mother is overcome by a feeling of impending tragedy. She is forced to deal not only with her premonition, but with the reactions of the other chaperons, her daughter, and finally with the near fatal accident that ensues.

HUMOR

A light touch can make almost any subject more publishable. "Heart Full of Love For Everyone," told of a young wife who took in temporary boarders from the local Humane Society and the disastrous result when her stuffy sister-in-law arrives for dinner at the same time as an orphaned puppy.

TIMELINESS

Subject matter that's in the news is always interesting. When the twin towers were falling over and over on TV, I, along with all my fellow Americans, was glued to the set. Finally, I realized that I had gone two days without doing a lick of work. I pulled a tablet and pen to the table in front of my TV and wrote the title "I Married a Terrorist" which I soon sold to *True Confessions*. It dealt with an Oklahoma girl marrying a man, a student at Spartan, the big aviation school in Tulsa, a man from an Arabic country. I allowed my surge of interest in a national happening to help me write a story that got quite a bit of fan mail, according to my then editor, Pat Byrdsong. The magazine only published two fan letters but I was thrilled with them. I wish the editors would publish more of the letters commenting on stories. I loved it in the days when all the letters were printed. Those letters give writers the feedback that is *almost* as important to us as money. Almost.

If nude scenes, love affairs, sex and variations on lust, leave you cold; If you'd rather educate than titillate, try a sex-less confession. It might be just what the editor is looking for to change the pace from her usual sexually charged love and/or deprivation of love stories.

CHAPTER 16: ELECTRONIC REQUIREMENTS

Writing and selling stories hot off your typewriter is still possible, but you're making life easier for yourself if you go ahead and spring for a computer and a printer.

True Confessions no longer depends on e-queries and e-submissions. The new editor at *True Confessions* and the other three *Trues* want hard copy but get this, they also want a disc of your story to accompany your confessions to their office. Now if you use a typewriter you're going to have to go and pay someone to scan your manuscript to make a disc for you to send... which means a lot of time, trouble and expense you could avoid by simply going electronic, specifically, Apple or Windows as your choices.

I also think that if you are a writer you *must* have a website. My website is www.peggyfielding.com. Please subscribe, and you will automatically receive a newsletter from me each month. Subscription is free, as you may already know. When I had zero computer knowledge, I thought you would have to pay for subscriptions to people's newsletters at their websites.

Dan Case, my editor at AWOC.COM, created my website. For a fairly reasonable fee he will do the same for you, I'd think. I am so ignorant electronically that I could no more build a website than I could build a car to drive. Let a professional put the website together for you.

Be sure your website builder (you or someone else) registers your domain name. If you have an easily remembered name or a fairly common Anglo Saxon type name, you may be too late to register it. Dan tells me he couldn't register as Dan Case or Daniel Case.com. They'd already been taken, if you can believe that.

Registration of your domain name will probably cost you something under $50.00.

Fear and loathing of my computer has been a hindrance to my career. Take some classes in usage from your local library, community college or your local high school. Many computer sales and repair businesses offer classes for a bit more money than is required by the public sector classes, but some sort of classes are probably required if you even approach my depth of electronic ignorance.

Or you can marry a computer expert. Believe me, you will need him or her rather frequently until you become proficient on your own. Sex doesn't even enter into it anymore so far as I am concerned but you could really get my interest piqued if you display a vast computer knowledge.

Since Dan already had a wife I am still leaning on friends and paid help. It really is dreadful to be so dumb and unknowledgeable about a skill that your job requires you to have and I've often wished to be 13 years old again and then I'd automatically *know* everything kids today know about computers.

Buy a computer and a printer. Buy paper and discs. Learn the required skills. You can do it. This dinosaur is doing it!

Dragging Peggy into the twenty first Century

CHAPTER 17: OTHER THINGS TO SELL TO THE CONFESSIONS MAGAZINES

There are a number of things you can write and sell to the confessions magazines other than the stories we've been discussing so far. Not a lot of money, but if they do take your stuff they pay you for them, and sometimes give you a byline.

NONFICTION ARTICLES

Nonfiction articles are not used in all the *Trues* all the time, nor in the black magazines either, but they do use some nonfiction some of the time. See the interview in chapter three with editor Nathasha Brooks-Harris for what black mags want. You'll need to study each of them for what they are interested in. *True Story* offers "My Visit From Beyond" almost every month and if they choose your article they'll pay you $100.00 for it. They'll print your name or initials with the story, as you choose. Manuscripts deal with paranormal happenings you've experienced. Your manuscript will not be returned or acknowledged but if you have a story about angels visiting you this is the place! Send it in.

Recipes are also used by several of the magazines and they give you a byline as well as pay you. A recent recipe page in *True Love* offered two pages of, "Oat Cuisine," with photographs. I believe they furnished the photographs.

"Women Are Wonderful," is another *True Story* department which takes nonfiction. Write about a woman who has had a positive influence on your life. They pay $50.00, no return on your manuscript, no acknowledgement.

Sometimes crafts stories are purchased if they are simple and illustrated. You also must send a finished example of the craft you describe.

POETRY

Poetry buys are fairly common now. I have seen poetry in all our magazines. Someone got paid for those verses. You just have to send poems that will appeal to this particular audience. They seem to like rhyme and sentimental, down-home works.

CONTESTS

When I first started writing and had zero income, I won a contest in *True Love*. They'd asked for stories about how we'd met our husbands. I was already divorced but couldn't see anything wrong with using the old boy one more time and telling the story of our first meeting. I was paid $25.00 for that bit. Thrilled? I guess so! I still don't turn up my nose at $25.00.

Each magazine has a series of contests that they run every month. Try for one of them. You may find you like it. And you may win "Reader of the Month" which wins $500.00. Now that's good money, my writer friends.

PHOTOGRAPHS

Mostly cute kids and cute animals. If you have cute shots of either kids or animals or both, check the magazines for what they're offering and then send your own color transparency (slide) and two or three lines explaining the picture and let yourself be paid for their right to print that picture of the cutest baby, cat, dog, in the world.

DON'T SEND ORIGINAL PHOTOGRAPHS! Have copies made because they won't send your entry back.

Just send your picture in slide format with a line or two of identification, then hope for the best. The staff at these magazines won't enter into any U.S. mail, email, or telephone discussions or conversations about your photograph nor about any of the other categories we've discussed in this chapter. Send this stuff out and forget about it!

YOU'RE COOKIN' IT COUNTRY WINNERS!

Many, many thanks to all of you who devored *True Story Family* members and dichard Loretta Lynn fans who sent in postcards to enter our recent You're Cookin' It Country cookbook giveaway, courtesy of author, coal miner's daughter, and greatly beloved music legend, Loretta Lynn, and the good people at Rutledge Hill Press. The response was *overwhelming* (postcards are *still* coming in from such far-flung places as Puerto Rico and Canada's Northwest Territories) *and* heartwarming, to say the very least! Basically, we learned two more wonderful things about *True Story* readers: 1) You *LOVE* fried chicken. 2) You love your moms even more!

Please join us in congratulating the 12 winners of brand-new copies of Loretta Lynn's delightfully entertaining and mouthwatering new cookbook, **You're Cookin' It Country!** Thanks to everyone who took the time to participate. Below, enjoy the winners' fond "memories of Mom," as written in their very own words.

Photo by Jeffrey Eisenberg

"I'm a coal miner's daughter, too! Born and raised in West Virginia for twenty-four years!"

Jackie M. Porter, Kansas:
"Mom's Best Meal: Country-fried

pie—all made from scratch."

Ms. Frankie Boyd, Arkansas:
"I had twelve brothers and sisters. The best thing I liked that Mom cooked was her pinto beans and cornbread. Sometimes we had fried potatoes. We were so thankful for everything we got."

Peggy Fielding, Oklahoma:
"My Mom's Best Meal: Ham hocks and pinto beans, green onions, sliced tomatoes, cornbread, iced tea, and blackberry cobbler (What *I* liked best!)."

Rose T. Lee, Arizona:
"Mom's Best Meal: Liver dumpling soup, roast capon, dumplings, peas, pumpernickel bread, and pumpkin pie."

Mrs. Georgia B. Crawford, Florida:
"Mom's Shepherd's Pie:
Brown large pkg. hamburger meat with onion and bell pepper.
Add 1 can beef gravy to beef, onion, and pepper mixture.
Pour into medium casserole dish and layer with: 1. 1 can whole kernel corn; 2. Mashed potatoes (leftover or fresh).
Top with 6 slices American cheese.
Heat oven to 350°. Bake till cheese is melted. Enjoy!

Alice J. Cline, New York:
"My mom was the best cook in the world—*my* world, at least! All of her meals were my favorites, *but* her special Spanish rice was a definite *favorite!*
She passed away three years ago at the age of ninety-two after seven years battling Alzheimer's. The last time she made my "favorite," she was in the end stages of the disease and when she went to pick up the casserole from the oven, she got a big burn on her arm because she'd "forgotten" how her oven worked. I'll never forget that meal she made for me and her determination to make it regardless of her health problems. She was truly one of a kind!"

Dolores R. DeWitt, Colorado:
"My mom made wonderful homemade bread and rolls—always won prizes for them. Mom's Best Meal: Fried chicken, mashed potatoes and gravy, homemade bread, homegrown green beans, and homemade cinnamon rolls. Yum, yum, yum!"

Lavonne DeRossett, Kentucky:
"My Mom's Best Meal: Southern fried chicken, cabbage coleslaw, creamed potatoes, no-bake pumpkin chicken, potato salad, hot rolls, and rice pudding."

Ms. Shirley Gross, Oregon:
"Mom's Best Meal: Baked macaroni and cheese, fried chicken, fresh corn-on-the-cob, fresh sliced tomatoes, and chocolate pie made with our cows' milk."

Christine M. Guillory, Louisiana:
"My Mom's Best Meal is every meal because she cooks them with love for us all. But my *favorite* meal is fried shrimp with French fries and macaroni and cheese with all of my brothers and sisters together, laughing and joking around the table."

Lori Byrd, Missouri:
"My Mom's Best Meal: Rolled pork roast, mashed potato dumplings, and sauerkraut with brown gravy over all, corn, biscuits, and apple crisp for dessert! The best!"

Jo Anne Sparrow, Illinois:
"My Mom's Best Meal was corn fritters, heavenly hash, and pineapple cream pie. My mom always made this on my birthday."

I won a Loretta Lynn cookbook from *True Story*

Peggy Moss Fielding

ABOUT THE AUTHOR

Photograph by Patricia Wade

Peggy Moss Fielding is a native Oklahoman who has spent several years outside the USA in Cuba, Japan, and the Republic of the Philippines. She lives in Tulsa, Oklahoma where she is a fulltime writer of both fiction and nonfiction. Fielding teaches writing part time at Tulsa Community College. Many of her former students have gone on to write and publish nonfiction books, novels, articles, short stories and confessions.

Fielding has published hundreds of articles, short stories and confessions as well as several nonfiction books and novels. She often speaks at Writer's conferences and seminars across the country.

Her website www.peggyfielding.com was put together for her by Dan Case, editor of the award-winning e-magazine, Writing for DOLLARS! http://www.WritingForDollars.com You may subscribe to Fielding's monthly newsletter on her website and/or to Writing for DOLLARS! Both free, of course.

Testimonials

Three authors who have profited from
Peggy's advice.

Selling to the Confessions Market
by Julie Williams

I took up writing as a hobby when I came to America from
England ten years ago. With my children grown and living in the
UK, I finally had the time to pursue something I'd always enjoyed.
At that time I wrote mostly children's stories and a few short
romances. I never thought of writing for the confessions market
until I heard Pat Byrdsong, (at that time) the Editor of True
Confessions speak at the Oklahoma Writers' Federation
Conference in 2004.

Pat opened my eyes to a world of possibilities if I wanted to
try it.

During her presentation, she made several references to Peggy
Fielding as a successful author who has written (and continues to
write) stories for this group of magazines. I found out that Peggy
had written a book on how to go about this subject, titled
*Confessing for Money (Writing and Selling to the Secret Short
Story Market)*.

I bought a copy and read it thoroughly.

Peggy has some wonderful tips in this book. I followed them. I
entered one story in a ByLine Magazine contest which had a
Confession genre category. The result, third place, showed me
that I do have what it takes to write a confession.

Buoyed by that success, I sent a different story to one of the
magazines Pat Byrdsong mentioned at the Conference and
"Second Chance" was accepted by *True Experience* for their fall
2005 edition.

It's a great thrill to know that many people (and not just one judge) will get to read my story and, hopefully, learn from it.

Peggy says this is an important aspect of writing for this market -- the fact that even if the person reading your story cannot identify completely with the character, they can at least learn from the character's experience and his/her choices. Should they ever be faced with a similar scenario in the future, they will know which decision to make.

Although ideas come easily to me, along with characters' names, at some point I do have to plot the storyline. Peggy has plenty of tips on how to do this and more, and I particularly like her formula for writing confessions. Wait until you see her illustration -- is it a shell, is it a wave? No, it's Peggy's drawing of a confession! And this works for most love stories, which also need their share of drama and conflict or else they are boring.

My first sale gave me a high, but I didn't just congratulate myself. I took Peggy's advice to start another right away rather than wait to hear back. Sometimes it takes several months before the story editor gets in touch. I was lucky - my response only took two weeks*.

In her book, Peggy also gives advice on manuscript preparation, office equipment, and how to keep records, etc. It is all useful information, and her tips for writing this genre, when used frequently, will become second nature.

I guess I broke a few rules the first time around, but I'm sure Peggy would say, "What are rules for if not to be broken?"

For instance, "Second Chance" is written from the man's point of view whereas the majority of Confessions type stories are from a woman's POV.

Secondly, it is set overseas, in Paris, and I've found from reading the stories that most take place in the US.

However, following Peggy's formula, my main character is pretty settled in his marriage but has made some bad decisions. He is about to make another critical one when an event takes place that causes him to think about his actions before it's too late.

But, staying true to the principles of these magazines, my story is based on an actual experience that I had in France. If I can turn a real-life event into a story, so can you.

Get Peggy's book and get writing.

Julie Williams

* Note: Julie's second story sold in just 3 weeks!

QUERIES MADE MY SALES
by Michele J. Rader

I confess that I've been writing these stories for several years now. After learning the techniques taught in Peggy's "Confessing For Money" course, I knew I could sell my stories. At first I wrote the whole 4,000-8,000 words from start to finish. I attached my hopes and dreams to each of my carefully honed creations and each one landed smack dab in a giant slush pile somewhere in New York City. After striking out many times, with averaging only about thirty-percent in sales, I decided to rethink my process of submission.

I met one of the editors at a writer's conference and immediately liked her. She had decided to accept email submissions* and invited those writers in attendance to send her queries. I constructed my query from the notes I had squirreled away in my "Great Ideas" Confessions notebook. With a short introduction about content and word count, I sent in my query and within a few weeks I had an answer.

Dear Michele,

Your story sounds interesting. Make sure to add plenty of emotion. I'll be looking forward to reading 'Internet Junkie'.

Sincerely, Pat

Now I had to get busy and write! Of course at this point my story was still under consideration, but with a positive response like that from an editor, I knew I had my foot in the door. So I wrote.

With each accepted story I sent, I also sent another query. Sometimes the editor would note that she already had several with that theme and asked me how I could give my story a different twist. Even if the new and improved version didn't fly, I had not spent the time and energy writing an entire story that wasn't hitting the magazine's needs.

Doing the footwork to see which editors accept queries not only saves time, but money in supplies and postage. Then next time I get out another of my Great Ideas, I hope to write a winning query that will make the editor respond, "I like that I idea. Send it in!"

Michele Rader

* Note: Just now none of the current editors at the "trues" accepts email queries. All prefer the completed story with disc sent via U.S. mail.

Breaking into the Confessions Market
by Pam Reeder

One of my goals in life was to become a published writer. One that was *PAID* for writing. Writing for the confessions market helped make that goal a reality.

I admit, reading confessions magazines was something I had not done since my teen years and then only a stray issue here and there when passed to me by an Aunt. So, writing for that market had not even entered my mind. And besides, I didn't have any deep dark secrets to confess. I lead a humdrum normal life, so I had nothing to offer the confessions market anyway. Boy was I wrong!

At our monthly writers' group meetings, writer after writer announced confession sales. And the confessions market was enthusiastically touted as the "hidden short story market." As I listened to them, my misperceptions about the confession magazines were set aright. It turns out stories didn't have to be about MY deep dark secrets or personal demons. They just had to be stories that were based on truth and could cover a broad spectrum of story lines. And it was such a hungry market it was in constant need. And it paid! Now, they really had my attention.

Thoroughly intrigued, I went to a confession writing workshop conducted by Peggy Fielding. This lady really knew the confessions market and was mentoring confession writers left and right. I became one of them. After just one class, and using the steps set out in her book "Confessing for Money", I wrote my first confession story and promptly sold it. Now that I knew the secrets of the confessions market, material for stories was everywhere. I went on to write three more stories back to back and they, too, were promptly purchased.

If you can respect the confessions market and are willing to write to its needs, Peggy Fielding's book *Confessing for Money* can help you break into writing short stories for the "paying" confessions market. That's why the book is called *Confessing for MONEY*.

Pam Reeder

CPSIA information can be obtained at www.ICGtesting.com
Printed in the USA
BVOW08s1239060214

344026BV00001B/204/P